The Dharma and The Hindu Castes

Jan Val Ellam

Lamp Publisher

The Dharma and the Hindu Castes
Copyright 2021 © Jan Val Ellam

All rights reserved. This book or any portion thereof may not be reproduced or used in any manner whatsoever, including mechanical, photocopying, or any information, storage, and retrieval system, without the express written permission from the publisher except for the use of brief quotations in a book review.

Printed United States of America
Lamp Publisher LLC

ISBN 978-1-7365834-0-1

Required Reflection:

Do yourself a favor: **Think!**

One more: **Decondition Yourself!**

Finally: **Set Yourself Free!**

Jan Val Ellam

The Dharma and The Hindu Castes

Contents

Lamp Publisher LLC forward a letter

The Dharma and the Hindu Castes.

We are pleased to publish one of Val Ellam's many books. We want to alert readers that we can permit ourselves to be free of dogmas that have imprisoned us.

We will immerse ourselves in a fantastic dive with panoramas never seen by today's humans. Our ancient texts like Bagavaghita, the Tora, the Bible, Greek Mythology, and others give us an unclear report of our history.

Val Ellam channels Entities that are out of this 3D existence. These Entities directly or indirectly claim that they were the progenitors of our range of reality or Matrix. Surprisingly, these Entities are giving another version of our history. The names and facts revealed will be out of our vocabulary, so we use Footnotes.

We came across Val Ellam's work in 2013. His works include many books and lots of hours of speeches. In 2016 we had a deep sense of reunion with the grateful joy of meeting Pandora. Val Ellam's channeled and published a book, *Pandora's Smile.*

Val Ellam warns us not to take his channeled information revealed as absolute truth. Find his Portuguese work at https://janvalellam.club.hotmart.com/login.

Lamp Publisher thinks that Val Ellam's channeled work is one of the most impressive fiction told. We are making a compilation of Val Ellam's Portuguese work and then translating it to English. Find out more about Pandora, The First Biological Mother of Humanity, at www.PandoraUnlock.com. The writers of history have suppressed Pandora's story. Pandora's intervention in the creation of the Homo-Sapiens on planet Earth changed its course forever.

Join us and find out who ended up opening Pandora's box.

Introduction

The Dharma[1] and Hindu C*astes.*[2]

Long before the curtains of the theater of life were opened so that human actors could begin to perform the mystery of their existences, other characters, currently unknown, had already performed here.

The director seemed to have started a project on this planetary stage but regretted it, and he never returned to finish.

Many intelligent beings that were here before humans acted accordingly to their way of understanding.

Humans have not been warned that several Demo[3] like people had dominated the terrestrial scene, and they had a strange existential discipline that had been created to put pressure on the educational order to which they were subjected. Much of what they did would later be mistakenly inherited by humans who apply a strange existential discipline on themselves until today.

Demo like people? Yes, because there were other classes of Demo like animals, Demo like vegetal beings, Demo like mineral beings, and so forth. They were made in pairs and in a crude way of existing.

---

[1] Dharma can mean "duty" even religion

[2] Castes or Varna are a hereditary transmission of a lifestyle that includes occupation, ritual status in a hierarchy and social interaction. They are a system that divided the society into 4 classes.

[3] Demo is breeding of beings that were created by the two gods of Trimurt, Shiva and Vishnu. We will have a surprise in the evolution of Homo genus.

Epic history, mysteries, and many mythological panels had taken us from those days when the Trimurti[4] created genus[5] of Demo that had their transition towards a humanization that was an unexpected process. They saw that this procedure would not be as expected because humans would never let themselves be dominated entirely. They criminally decided to condition and influence the new Homo[6] genus, the future Homo Sapiens.

The veil started to unfold, and we could have a glimpse of a terrible mistake. In that time occurred a misunderstanding, a system of procedures and strict laws designed for the Demo with their specific behavior. They were probably in need of such behavior correction, which was applied to humans and turned into an unfortunate habit.

May one day the reflections showed here to be useful to the beloved brothers and sisters and whoever goes through the land of India. In this my lifetime, India is a country that I could visit in the year 2000. I visit Mumbai (formerly Bombay), Bangalore, Puttaparthi, and the surroundings.

---

[4] Trimurti the 3 gods creators: Bhrama the Creator, Vishnu the Preserver and Shiva the Destroyer.

[5] Genus is any breeding group that has genetic characteristics in common.

[6] Homo is another breeding of being that were created by the two gods of Trimurti, Shiva and Vishnu. We will have a surprise in the evolution of Homo genus to Homo Sapiens.

I went to India to study Hinduism and see the practice of Vedic culture, of Ahimsa[7], and, mainly, to check the level of influence of the Upanishads[8] - philosophical comments about the Vedas[9] - in the life of the middle-class Hindu. At that time, I observed people, talked to some local traders, and visited the Sai Baba ashram[10].

Atlan, May 4th of 2018

Jan Val Ellam

[7] Ahimsa is much more than non-physical, mental or emotional violence, it is the liberation from the cycle of reincarnation. Avoiding offending any living being. Ahimsa in the Hindu tradition and others tradition is the respect for all living things and avoidanca of violence toward others.

[8] Upanishad "Sanskrit" is to practice to purity and serenity. To prepare to study about God and its nature. It is late Vedas.

[9] Vedas "Sanskrit" most ancient Hindu scriptures which was directly revealed by the seers among the early Aryans in India. Preserved by oral tradition.

[10] Sai Baba Indian Guru and philanthropist resided much of the time in his mains ashram

1. The Dharma Factor

The word Dharma hides many mysteries in itself and in the context in which it arose. Although many think they understand it deeply.

In my life, I faced intriguing aspects. I had to coexistence with the Entity known as Lord of Dharma, the same self-proclaimed Lords of Lila[11], from the Hindu Trimurti – I began to suspect one thing. If Dharma were the mental panel on which those beings learned to compose all the interpretations that modern knowledge has about what is considered the Hindu Holy Vedas, these needed to be revised.

In the book written in Portuguese, *The Art of Saving* by Nilton Bonder[12] , the dialogue between a disciple and a rabbi the disciple says:

> I have been struggling for twenty years and have not achieved the reaching of a craftsman who

---

[11] Lila "Sanskrit" The 3 gods of Trimurti discovered that they could not destroy each other, their battles only brought confusion and destruction. Lila was created to reduce confusion and allow for some creation. Game play!

[12] Nilton Bonder; Rabbi, born in Brazil, 1957.

> becomes a master of his art, either by creating something of better quality or something that is done more efficiently and quickly. As it was twenty years ago, so I am today.
>
> The rabbi then replied, "Take the case of an ox, for example. Every morning, it leaves it is stable, goes to the field, plows the land, and is taken back to its stable. This is done day after day, and nothing changes concerning the ox – however, each year, the plowed land yields its harvest."

Nilton Bonder comments that any diploma does not celebrate our life when we complete the envisioned curriculum. In the above citation itself, life does not celebrate but rejoices in its fields.

He concludes by saying that the disciple's desire to be perfecting himself as if he were sculpting himself as an illusion. It is the plowed fields, meaning the things we did, that will have an impact on ourselves and the world.

Disagreements aside from this last statement, I emphasize the most crucial aspect for me here in the 1st Verification.

1st Verification

Universal life seems to use the bee, the ox, man, and everything else that is alive to take advantage of the achievements that each portion of particularized consciousness, rationalized or not, sculpts in the electrons that constitute their bodies, their way of expression.

The immortal electron seems to be forced to move, carrying the information since the beginning it absorbs in its

quantum capacity to assimilate and record "everything" it has experienced since the first micro instant of Universal Creation.

Where is this information directed to? The day black holes will be better understood, even by scientists; we can start to figure out the universe's creation. The knowledge produced in the biological universe will be passed on to the Demo universe. In universal life, everything changes because of shrinkage[13], among other forces.

The temporal universe in which we live will exist until the hydrogen[14] supply ends. And the last star of the cosmos goes out. The electron will continue collecting everything it can experience through bodies such as spiders, frogs, lions, and more complex rationalized beings (the terrestrial human, for example); scientists point to be a universal emerging mind.

From this perspective – and this is one reason I'm afraid I have to disagree with Nilton Bonder's statement. He believes that man does not sculpt anything in himself by producing his best or worst content for life – the subject becomes extraordinarily deeper.

The most enlightened Hindus' current belief defines Dharma as the sacred duty of each being. However, the point is that the broader context in which this concept is inserted concerns a specific time. When it was created by

---

[13] Shrinkage's universe is guaranteed by the force called Shiva's raja that will make it disappear. Shiva is the third god in the Hindu triumvirate.

[14] Hydrogen and helium, were produced in the hot, dense conditions of the birth of the universe irself, about 14 billion B.C.E.

an avatar[15] called Krishna[16] and applied as a factor of political and social organization for a singular race, these intermediate races come from a particular genetic segment of some classes of non-human beings, who were considered gods and semi-gods – and men.

2nd Verification

Thirteen million years ago, there was great devastation. Several non-human people belonged to a type of gender that currently no longer exists. This type of genus was derived from some descendants of different physical genetics – Demo genetics – who roamed planet Earth for a long time while their portals[17] were still open[18], allowing that kind of transit.

The beings were originally antimaterial; their body was created with a type of material that made them natural inhabitants of this biological universe for a specific time. Their bodies could not be easily classified as such if compared to humans.

Although many of them have no sex organs and have an active biological aspect in their body forms, there is something else in terms of the vital circuit and neural possibilities in their brains, which has caused mental conventions that somewhat differed from those that are currently perceived in humans.

---

[15] Avatar "Sanskrit" is an energy expressed in the form of a being created by the gods of Trimurti to represent them.

[16] Krishna avatar for the Trimurti; Brahma, Vishnu and Shiva.

[17] Portals doorway, gate, entrance to connect physical world end spirit, parallel, extraterrestrial realms.

[18] Open today the portals are closed and they are working to find a way to open it again.

Their genetic areas were much more focused on the expression of the demonic mental power than existing and preponderant in many of the phases of an unknown universal history for humans, which were compiled[19] as a Demo culture[20]. For the time being, unknown to humanity, even though many of its faces are registered in what humans call mythology. These algorithms allowed expressions of the Demo type's power and were deeply strange to humans' patterns today consider acceptable or normal.

This race of demigods, whose biodemol pattern[21], adorned with the Homo characteristics, was the culmination of this existential genus and ended up specifying[22] – in simple language, it is when a species mutates and generates subspecies from its original genome – in many people that have spread across the legendary Hyperborean[23] continent, in the far north, in northern Europe and Asia, and some later also settled further south.

---

[19] Compiled – The Demo compile their history in order to preserve their memory.

[20] Demo culture is the name they gave for their compilation.

[21] Biodemol pattern formed by irrational, asexual, and non-operative beings for universal progress like vegetables as an example.

[22] Specifying this word is being used with the sense that the human being can adapt in any environment. For example, if he goes to live in an environment without gravity, he may mutate and have more arms than legs, because he will not be able to walk.

[23] Hyperborean mythical people according to the ancient Greeks, they lived for 1,000 years.

To better organize those hybrid ethnicities, Lord Krishna consummated something that Manu[24] – someone who lived well before him – had long ago adopted for his contemporaries. The ancestors of these hybrid beings, which was the concept of organization of a Demo Homo society that stood out for dividing individuals in accordance with the Varna,[25] that at that time, meant the mark of each being, the leading natural talent of an entity with some Demo pattern in its genome.

According to Hindu traditions, Manu was the great mentor and legislator of humankind, also called Manu Vaivasvata[26], considered the progenitor of the human species, a son of Surya, one of the gods of the Vedic pantheon.

Some studies suggest Manu would correspond to Adam, or even one of his descendants mentioned in his biblical lineage unfolded, known as Seth, Enos, Caiman, Malalahel, Jared, Enoch, Methuselah, Lamech, Noah, following up with Abraham and his descendants.

While a human being can present the richness of displaying multiple talents and express them well, **Demo being before hybridization could only carry a specific talent that identifies them with the ones of their kind.**

The Demo genus beings were created fully developed with power but somehow demented. They were

---

[24] Manu" Sanskrit" has several meanings as the Lord of the Land, The man architect.

[25] Varna or Caste "Sanskrit" has several meaning including was used to refer to social classes.

[26] Vaivasvata the seventy Manu.

ethereal beings and could metamorph. Metamorph means that they could transform their appearance.

The beings were created in some kind of cocoon. The birth process that we know as today's humans, at that time it had not yet been developed. The Demo composed their society with Castes or Varnas, which gave them the fulfillment of their logic and helped them get greater effectiveness in their contribution to the community.

Let's take a look at the 4 main Varna systems.

Shudras are the Artisans and Unskilled Workers.
Vaishyas are Farmers, Merchants, and Business People.
Kshatriyas are Warriors, Police, and Administrators.
Brahmanas are Priests, Teachers, and Intellectuals.
https://iskconeducationalservices.org/HoH/practice/dharma/the-four-varnas/. Site referred

Let's take another look at Bhagavad Gita[27] script passages.

It is better to perform one's prescribed duties, even though faulty than another's duties. Destruction in the course of performing one's own duty is better than engaging in another's duties, for to follow another's path is dangerous.

Bhagavad Gita 3.35

---

[27] Bhagavad Gita is among the most important religious texts of Hinduism and the best known some times refered as Gita. It is a 701 verse Hindu scripture that is part of the epic Mahabharata.

> Brahmanas, Kshatriyas, Vaishyas, and Shudras are distinguished by the qualities born of their own nature in accordance with the 3 material qualities.
>
> Bhagavad Gita 18.41

In this way, the Demos organized themselves into a system of Castes or Varnas to fulfill their Dharmas, and everything is written in their historical Vedic religion, or ancient Hinduism. During the late Vedic period (1100-500 B.C.E), Brahmanism develops out of the Vedic religion. These ideas and practices are found in the Vedic texts, and some Vedic rituals are still practiced today.

After hybridization, Demo Homo[28] beings should accomplish their duties or Dharma, focusing on the good of the community, where they combine their contributions around everyone's progress.

Everyone who? The hybrid ethnicity beings!

When humans set out to appear in Creation, their development was entirely different scenery. They were more like animals than fully beings with rights. The animals did not belong to the Castes or Varnas or have Dharma.

[28] Demo Homo is a kind of hybridization of Demo and Homo Sapiens by the time maybe Neanderthal and/or Cromayon.

Let’s take a look at Homo Sapiens’ chart evolution, the future Humans of today

Figure 1

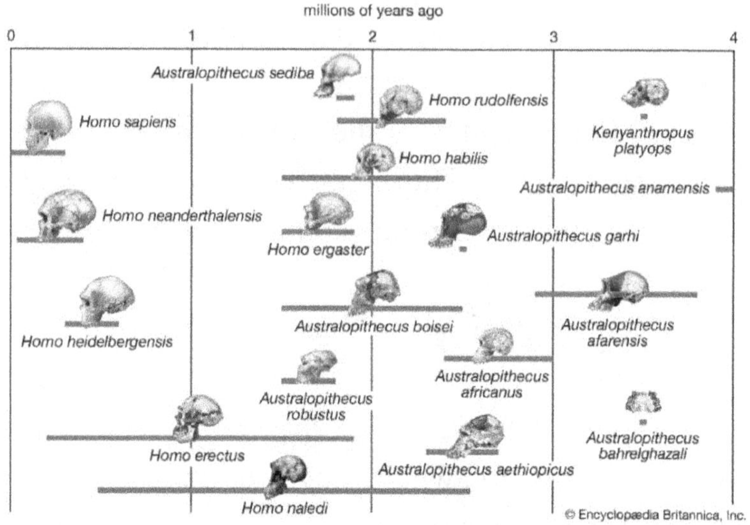

Possible pathways in the evolution of the human lineage.

Image: Encyclopedia Britannica, Inc.

In those days, powerful hybrid beings thought they would inherit the Earth and have Humans as pack animals, pets, or as a brute force for their armies, or in the future to mine and on and on. They did use the animals at that time with the same psychological tranquility that we do today.

The Dharma of each Caste was the sacred duty. The method was available and possible to be applied at that time. Then, emerged much product of the association of Demo genetics with another, and with being of extraterrestrial order, both of which are already crossbred with the genetics with the men and women who began to occupy their spaces on the periphery of the progress of those powerful hybrid beings.

The Dharma pedagogical model was established in the past and, finally, introduced in some Demo classes and their descendants, or hybrid unfolding, subject to evolution.

Today, humans understand Dharma as an honor, and it was in honor of the accomplished Dharma or accomplished sacred duty, the peace and satisfaction of the evolved Demo psyche.

Why is Dharma the only way psychologically possible to trigger and evolve the Demo mind?

The answer will seem simple but, only in the future, this subject can be better understood and strengthen.

In the Demo genome, or at least in many of its classes, there is a trigger where their mental area can be moved or modified and evolved. The feelings of pride, vanity, presumption, and arrogance, among other sickly, affected aspects of the demonic mind, are malformed.

The issue of personal Demo honor has been long crafted to be taken over by worthy Demos deserving to be thought of as gods by the least warned entities.

In the *Mahabharata*[29] itself, we see an episode that, for human logic, would be absolutely unacceptable, but,

---

[29] *Mahabharata* and *Ramayana* are the two majors Sanskrit epics of ancient India.

for the Demo culture, it was and is the right side of the story. Because from their point of view, a given word cannot go back.

Extravagant, the honor present in those beings' psyche, forced them never to go back on anything said, so valuable was the spoken word. For this reason, in the Mahabharata, Queen Kunti's case is narrated, which, under what she expressed thinking that it was another matter, ended up determining and requiring all her Pandavian[30] sons had to share the same wife, named Draupadi.

Excess? It may seem to us, but not for the way of life of those beings.

In the *Mahabharata*, by the author Krishna Dharma, page 54.

Kunti[31] waited alone at the hut for her sons to return. She felt anxious. What if they had been discovered? Duryodhana and his brothers would undoubtedly be on the swayamvara[32]. If they saw the Pandavas alive, then they would certainly try to have them killed. Kunti remembered Vyasadeva's predictions. Surely that illustrious sage could not have been wrong. But the course of destiny was always difficult to fathom. The Supreme Lord was the ultimate controller – and no one could know his plan.

Kunti busied herself in preparing her sons' evening meal. As she bustled about the hut, she suddenly heard Arjuna[33]'s voice

---

[30] Pandavian the 5 brothers' sons of Pandu, the king of Hastinapur.

[31] Kunti, also known as Pritha is one of the most impotant female protagonist of the epic, *Mahabharata*.

[32] Swayamara wa a practice of choosing a husband, from among a list of suitors, by a girl of marriageable age.

[33] Arjuna one of the 5 Pandava brothers, who are heroes at *Mahabharata*.

greeting her. “Dear mother, we are back. Come and see the wonderful alms we have got today”.

Feeling a surge of relief, Kunti called back, “I am so glad you are safe. Share the alms equally among you.”

Arjuna then entered the hut with Yudhishthira[34]. Draupadi[35] came with them, and when Kunti saw her, she was shocked. “Oh! What have I said?” The Kuru queen felt her religious principles threatened. She values truth above everything. Even in jet, she would not speak a falsehood. But she had said that all her sons should share Draupadi. How was it possible? No woman could have five husbands. She looked anxiously at Yudhishthira.

“Do not worry, mother,” Yudhishthira replied. “You shall doubtlessly be saved from sin.”

Yudhishthira and Arjuna, “You have won this maiden, and thus you should now take her hand in sacred marriage.”

Arjuna looked at his brother in honor. “Please do not cast me onto the path of wicked men. What virtuous man would accept a maiden’s hand in the presence of his unmarried elder brother? You should be the one to marry her, not me. After that should come to Bhima[36], and only then myself, and finally the twins.”

By now, the other Pandavas had entered the hut, and hearing Arjuna’s words, they all glanced at Draupadi, who smiled and returned their looks. All 5 brothers felt their hearts leap, and their minds become bewildered. The Panchala princess glowed with beauty, and she filled the hut with her natural bodily fragrance. The brothers could hardly take their eyes away from her.

Seeing the condition of his brothers, Yudhishthira feared that Draupadi may cause disunion among them. After reflecting for some moments, he then said, “This chaste girl shall become the wife of us

---

[34] Yudhishthira is the first among the 5 Pandava brothers.
[35] Draupadi is the common wife of the 5 Pandava brothers.
[36] Bhima is the second among the 5 Pandavas.

all. This is our mother's order, and in my view, it is what Vyasadeva meant when he told us of her destiny."

The brother's ha wondered about the sage's words, but how they understood. All of them felt great joy. Draupadi was a prize beyond compare.

In another version of *Mahabharata* – there are several of them – the same episode has some variations.

Judeo-Christian logic, currently westernized by Catholicism, will never understand how much of the apparent mystery exists behind the narratives of the Mahabharata, which will always seem more fictional to us. However, it is not!

3rd Verification

These translations are recent and replete with the inevitable religious anthropomorphism.

The beings Demos and Demo Homo that were created from the fire had been transformed into men, women, boys, and girls when they were not in reality. This is the creation of Brahma or Yahweh.

The human beings in the molds that we know today ran outside or saying it better. They live their lives in parallel to what is described in the Mahabharata.

Human involvement took place without the dominant forces giving any importance to the fact that they exist.

In those times, Krishna's mission, a Keshava[37] avatar sent by the 3 Lords of Trimurti, was here to try to carry out the measures of the last historical stages, which had been envisioned. He had a plan for the beings who were here and who would finally inherit the land. Krishna and everybody else did not expect that the Homo Sapiens would end up inheriting the blue planet.

4th Verification:

This background of the story described in the pages of the Mahabharata was not even understood by the Aryan ancestors themselves. They witnessed it in a certain way, much less by Hinduism, who inherited and absorbed it as a story of gods, demigods, and others, making a mistake in the final translation of the facts when classifying them like human beings.

The issue was further complicated as ancestral translators' humans recorded in writing the oral tradition. These ancestors definitely transformed into a human epic when that aspect does not correspond to what truly happened. This story has nothing to do with humans.

Vyasa, the author of the *Mahabharata* and the group, was never humans, but it looked like it did not have been noticed, which is s a big mistake.

In the *Mahabharata*, unfortunately, the Demo honor aspect is explored in the narratives, but it is not explained

---

[37] Keshava is a way for a being to express its energy that can be an avatar or any other expression.

why those postures are so valued, nor the reason for the extreme zeal and zest of its practice.

This is because the Demo honor, so hardly built-in its limited psychism – disfigured as it could or can be considered by the human eye – It was the basis of Demo ethics on what the Castes issue was established for the education of a genus which destiny appeared to be that of inheriting the Earth.

From my unfortunate coexistence with the Trimurti beings, I can testify that they thought these hybrid beings would inherit the Earth, which was precisely what they wanted. But they had a huge surprise.

Demo ethics? Yes, because all ethics brings with it a psychic-mental-cultural convention that allows a giant cell of coexistence, whether in family, group, municipal, regional, national, or even worldwide, to exist in foundations compatible with the position of its members or social agents. The Demo did not escape this, quite the contrary, and we humans inherited these conventions from them.

5th Verification

For the Demo, as mentioned earlier, the logic of the greater effectiveness of each being's contribution to the community, associated with the concept of Varna, to succeed, it was necessary that this individual contribution was linked to the notion of personal honor as a way of guaranteeing rectitude of personal conduct.

The Demos thought they were immortal; then they performed their duties for the contribution of the Caste they belonged. Demos did not glimpse the issue of the future awards or punishment of Karma. But it was precisely what happened because the intermediaries between Demo and current humans arose, and they become mortal beings. Today, humans have the concept of reincarnation or future lives and become part of karma judgment or punishment from past lives.

The Karma would naturally establish itself for individualized consciousness according to how the expression of personal Dharma is always linked to that of the Caste to which it belonged.

Unfortunately, the Demo honor, observing with the critical eyes of the human logic of the present, suffers from the absence of a portion of common sense. Dharma and Castes issue that comes in the future was not foreseen.

6th Verification:

To further guarantee the faithful fulfillment of personal Dharma in Castes its roots, it is linked to what had become known today as religion. The Demo believes it was assimilated as the fear of someone supposedly superior.

Imagine! The Homo Sapiens conditioning was total.

The justification that these beings gave us for things to be that way was so shocked. I was reluctant to produce this book for fear of disfiguring their explanations. I have a non-conformity, and philosophical rejection offered to these so-called gods – since some of them are still considered gods by many of the humans who venerate them. Frankly, it is not my case; even dough great is my effort not to despise them.

This is how I express myself, and I want to make it clear that much of what I will record here. It has to do with my disillusioned awareness of any romanticized aspect concerning the hidden reality unaware to today's humans. My disillusion comes during my coexistence with beings that seem to represent forces that intend to dominate us and have worked on this for a long time.

According to them, at some point in human history, precisely in these more recent times, they gave up such domination attempts, handing it over to destiny and human free will. I have my doubts!

In any case, according to them, domination is for the good. In my view, they make use of the human species as a mere biological experiment in progress – in the same way, that we use our brothers, the animals of terrestrial nature, for our laboratory experiments.

They, the gods, also claim to be our brothers and, more than that, our progenitors!

Whatever the truth is there, I clearly think I know from the facts that humans, in their Aryan/Hindu cultural tradition, inherited the Caste system. The system now weighs on their shoulders of our Hindu brothers and sisters.

However, this was not always the case. Since the current Hindus were not the first humans to inherit such outgrowth, seen under the eyes of modernity. Even though someone, like Sai Baba, clearly demonstrated no excess in the organizational method of human societies, I will refer to this in another chapter.

Brahma's first try of a lineage to be chosen was a grandson of Noah's Heber through his firstborn descendent, Shem. In a more remote time, he chooses the Aryans, descendants of Gomer, son of Japheth, his second choice.

The Creator Brahma – said to the descendent of Noah that he would have one of his descendent represent him on Earth and he would be called Yahweh - at a certain point in his attempt to regain control over the human race. Since the disengagement that the minds of Adam and Eve had gone through. Yahweh chose to deny the lineage of the descendants of the so-called biblical patriarchs. As follows: Adam, Set, Enos, Cainan, Malalahel, Jared, Enoch, Methuselah, Lamech, Noah, Sem, Asfarxad, Salé, Héber, Faleg, this genetic sequence goes on supposedly until the time of Abraham.

Gomer's descendants who came to be known as Aryans. The Caste weight had a direct inheritance to Gomer. Brahma, Vishnu, and Shiva, the 3 Trimurti gods, decide to test the Caste system among humans. That Caste system was totally different from the social organization that Noah and his descendants had practiced.

In the end, Hindus inherited the Caste system from Aryans. The question of heredity in this story is so deplorable that even Nazism would emerge in recent times due to the genetic game behind the unsuspecting human ethnicities.

7th Verification

Only when the Aryans, long after Gomer, migrated towards the Indian subcontinent, their crossbreeding with the Dravidians[38] and transferred the Castes' heritage to current Hindu traditions' roots. Dravidians were inhabitants of Harappa and Mohenjo Daro's ancient civilizations, which ruins currently belong to Pakistani territory.

What bluntly confuses the sense of this afflicted scribe is the level of conditioning. And more precisely, of the current our Hindu brothers and sisters. They seem not to perceive not to take it seriously. The fact that the gods, demigods, and other idols, whom they worship, all of them are from Demodharmic origin. I need to remind everyone that by the time Demo was developed, good or bad did not exist. Even so, these beings are seen as possessing human nature and logic, factors that have never been part of their psyche, and this aspect is, in my view, the most embarrassing misinterpretation of Hinduism in general.

For what reason is it up to a Western man of my size, I mean an ordinary man like me. I have to build a new

[38] Dravidians were descendants of neolithic farmers who predominantly speack any of the Dravidian languages.

way of looking at the very old and ancient Hindu mythology and its historical genesis and questions. This is a doubt that bothers me deeply.

I have to give a new meaning to what is considered the ancient Hindu's reality. Hindus practice worshiping beings as if they were gods. That never was the case. They were only non-human beings who ended up generating us. There is an aspect that only the future can clarify. However, when it comes to India and its millenary history, it seems that nothing normal fits it, which makes the hidden to be somehow revealed to the understanding of today. In order that we can be better realize what is, apparently, taken as incomprehensible.

2. The Trimurtian Castes

In order to try to understand the incongruity of the Caste system and the circumstances in which it arose. I think it is necessary to draw a historical panel of the chronology events that occurred in the past. Officially unknown, the ancestors of the Aryans who, later, transmitted their legacy to Dravidians/Hindus.

As far as I am aware, the Caste system first appeared on Earth in two focus of non-human clusters. One is located among the Hyperborean people in the North. Another one from the Kumari Kandan[39] tradition, in southern India, in lands that, at that time (about 20 thousand years B.C.E), connected the south of the Indian continent. The current island of Sri Lanka did belong to it, but the ocean's rising later covered that.

Newly archaeological discovered and the whole set of mythological history, these two civilizing foci remain officially unknown even doubt there are local traces of their existence.

---

[39] Kumari Kandan was first used to describe Lemuria in the 1930s, or Kingdom of the Earth.

The fact is that the developments of the Hyperborean people, a descendant of Gomer, got involved – Gomer is Noah's grandson and ancestors of the Aryans. Later came another wave of migration, the Aryans as being Indo-European[40]. The Caste system would reach the inhabitants of the Saraswati civilization, from which the kingdom of Bharata, now known as India, would emerge.

The official history unknown the Aryans formation because the frontier that separates them simply does not exist by that time. No orthodoxy can resist the archaeological discoveries that are happening in the Indian continent, especially on its border with Pakistan. These point to cities whose existences are well before what the orthodox view intends to accept as to be the time when humans started to take an active part in the terrestrial panorama.

It is exactly about these archaeological sites, and in what has been revealed in them, I will now try to catch the reader's attention.

At the end of the 20th century, the dry riverbed of an extinct river, surrounded by myths, was discovered via satellite. In this way, the legendary Saraswati[41] River either resurfaced for scientific knowledge or was rediscovered off the Indus river valley, where the

---

[40] Nineteenth-century **European** scholars used the term Aryan to identify the **Indo-European** or **Indo**-Germanic peoples who settled throughout India, Persia (Iran), and **Europe** thousands of years earlie

[41] Saraswati river 6000 years ago the river disappeared due to tectonic disturbance.

Saraswati-Sindhu[42] civilization developed around 5,000 years ago.

According to the study, it was due to geological and climatic changes that this river dried up around 4,000 years ago. The rediscovery of this river forced the scholars to reinterpret the disappearance of the civilization that, until then, had existed in this region.

Previously, it was thought that it had been destroyed because of an alleged invasion by the Aryans. However, it is now believed that local climate change, which transformed the region into a desert, was the cause of this civilization's decline.

Why is it important? The Vedic tradition forms the basis of all Hindu beliefs – but it started when the current Hindus didn't even exist – originated precisely in that Saraswati-Sindhu civilization, now lost in the mists of time. The system of Castes, as we know it today, has to do directly with this civilization.

To better situate which until now, it is not accepted historical context around the issue of Caste. I will divide the chronology of the facts into Pre-Vedic, Vedic, and Post-Vedic Eras – as do the most advanced studious of the subject – since it is at the heart of the Vedic teachings that the Castes arose.

---

[42] Saraswati-Sindhu civilization flourished circa 4000 to 1700 B.C.E on the river valleys of Indus and Sarasvati rivers. The drying-up of river led to migrants.

The formulation of these teachings appeared, for our analysis, as a central issue in the entire cultural process that gave and supports the absurd Caste system when observed by today's eyes. Unfortunately, however, the context is not that simple.

I take this opportunity to reaffirm that judging the past with the present's eyes is always an inglorious and even unproductive task—the results of the analyses made, starting from what currently seems to be noticeable. However, the obvious of the present often does not serve the past that is being evaluated, and this is the case of the Castes in its origin.

The Castes were based on the concept of Dharma, which Hindus have always cultivated since they received it as an inheritance from the Aryans who migrated to the south, built on the personal talent of the Demo and organized according to the interest of collective progress.

This cultural concept of Dharma linked to the Castes' sacred duty was passed on from generation to generation, being itself the guiding thread of the personal values of the Hinduism faithful ones.

Historically, as already stated, it seems to have come from the Saraswati civilization – which is the oldest that appears among the mists of this distant past, from the perspective of Hindu mythology – one of the foci of the start of the Caste system implementation among non-human beings, which implies, here, to register that, perhaps, let us again speak about the result of the beginning of the branches migration of the Hyperborean hybrid people's offspring who, in successive waves, were approaching the temperate zones and also the tropical zones.

From this perspective, the foci of the Caste system genesis are mixed, which could have influenced the Aryan migration, a local increase from another Hyperborean flow. Much many occurred; indeed, the topic is a controversial subject among the studious. However, for what we intend to focus on in this book, whatever the truth of those days is, it does not alter the thesis presented here, as both ratify the genesis of a first non-human hour in implementing the social Caste organizing system in ancestral communities.

By that time, humans, already thinkers, associated themselves with the most powerful community nucleus, transforming themselves into slaves or even into intelligent pets. Apart from these, there were only scattered tribes of humans who systematically fled these beings considered to be powerful.

The few humans of these tribes, who achieved a high degree of independence and even knowledge, were persecuted and rarely respected and kept close to the nucleus of power.

In these times of Saraswati civilization – that we can consider as being pre-Vedic, but already post-flood – the first era began, worthy of being considered the origin of Aryan mythology, which was later transformed into one of the ancestral stages of the history of India.

This ancestral stage – actually occurred in lands in Asia, around the Indian subcontinent – would be associated with another, which occurred only more recently, in which the late migration of other Aryan people was made in the same direction as that of their ancestors.

This aspect differs from what the historical avant-garde of today's Hindu studious defend as the historical truth they are proposing as a way of replacing the unacceptable and anachronistic view that the West imposed on the genesis of Indians, of a more recent process, when this took place in very remote times, not even considered as effectively historical.

Thus, this so-called Pre-Vedic Era, which duration was estimated to have occurred between 6,500 to 9,000 years ago, was marked by the emergence of this unique civilization located between the Indu and Saraswati rivers, the latter of which currently does not exist.

According to several Hindu authors of today, the Saraswati civilization was not only the oldest on the planet, but it was also the largest of high antiquity, much larger than Summer, Assyria, and Egypt combined.

It is known today that, at least 5,000 years B.C.E, this civilization extended over an area of about 750 thousand square kilometers.

According to the information I have, coming from living with beings out of the Matrix who control the annals of news about these times – most of which records were all destroyed and others lost – around that time, in the lands of Turkey, Noah and his descendants began to spread across the planet. Also, in northern Europe, other branches of Hyperborean decedents they established there. Later they descend towards the south direction as a way of adapting to milder climates.

It is important to understand that, just as one of the nuclei of the descendants of Noah went through the Caste experience (the descendants of Gomer), other descendants of Hyperborean migrations also experienced the implementation of the Caste system even at the time when non-human beings were the majority of those population centers.

Lord Krishna worked on his mission in many places, and a more significant presence of himself in the Saraswati civilization appears to have existed a Demo style intelligence center or a control center on the Caste system.

Traditionally, it is said that Brahmins were born from Brahma[43], from his head, a class composed of priests and scholars, who represent about 15% of the Indian population. From Brahma's arms, the Kshatriyas, who were warriors and defenders of Dharma, today politicians, and the military. Form Brahma's legs the Vaishyas, merchants, landowners. From Brahma's feet, he Sudras a vast class formed by servants, workers in general who until recently were not allowed to have contact with Hindu teachings. Outside this Caste system are the untouchables, the outcasts, which would have arisen from the dust under

---

[43] Brahma is the Hindu creator god and know by Christians as Yahweh.

Brahma's feet, such as Dalits, who are outside the organization of the Indian population represented by the Castes. Those who violated the Caste system by breaking the rules of Hindu society also become outcasts.

8th Verification:

The DNA of Brahma/Yahweh is a basis used to build a life, both Demo and Human. Using the reference to Brahma's head, arms, legs, and feet is just a modern way of representing his DNA, and it is saying that it belongs to him.

In much older times, however, when the Sun and its planets did not even exist, we can find a strange story I Neil Gaiman[44], author of the book *Norse Mythology*, page 32.

It was time for the creation of everything. Ve and Vili, and Odin looked at each other and spoke of what was needful to do, there is the void of Ginnungagap. They spoke of the universe, and of life, and of the future.

Odin and Vili and Ve killed the giant Ymir. It had to be done. There was no other way to make the worlds. This was the beginning of all things, the death that made all life possible.

They stabbed the great giant. Blood gushed out from Ymir's corpse in unimaginable quantities; fountains of blood as salt as the sea and gray as the oceans gushed out in a flood so sudden, so powerful, and so deep that it swept away and drowned all the giants. (Only one giant, Bergelmir, Ymir's grandson, and his wife survived by clambering onto a wooden box, which bore them like a boat. All the giants we see and we fear today are descended from them.)

[44] Neil Gaiman is an English Author.

Odin and his brothers made the soil from Ymir's flesh. Ymir's bones they piled up into mountains and cliffs.

Our rocks and pebbles, the sand and gravel you see: these were Ymir's teeth, and the fragments of bones that were broken and crushed by Odin and Vili and Ve in their battle with Ymir.

The seas that girdle the worlds: there were Ymir's blood and sweat.

Look up into the sky: you are looking at the inside of Ymir's skull. The stars you see at night, the planet, all the comets, and the shooting stars, these are the sparks that flew from the fires of Muspell. And the clouds you see by day? There were once Ymir's brains, and who knows what thoughts they are thinking, even now.

The dismantling of the Primordial Being's body represents the dramatic line of what, later, Vedism used to implement the Caste system adopted by current Hinduism.

Although, in particular, I criticize the common understanding of translations regarding Norse Mythology. The giant Ymir translates the most basic essence of the genesis of the Caste system, explained as having originated from distinct codes of the same body.

9th Verification:

Because the original body that they are talking about here is that of the Creator Brahma. All beings born into existence within the scope of his Creation must necessarily have his secret DNA source code as the basis of their bodies.

For the critical eyes of those that see us from outside, we are just animals that have acquired a strange and unfathomable nature – was an honest way of saying, between the lines with the knowledge of then, that the Creator's source code is present in all bodies.

The fact is that, due to the deepening of anthropological and archaeological studies, among other areas of scientific research, that were produced since the middle of the 19th century, when several essential ruins were discovered and correctly classified, the temporal issue and other aspects of classical view began to fall off their false pedestals of established truths.

The excavations that were still being carried out on the past's dust have unveiled disturbing panels to maintain the current classical view that historians have about those forgotten times.

Cities that are considered legendary emerge in broad daylight, whether from desert sands or even ocean waters, as is the case with Dwarka[45], attesting that the legendary and mythological past starts demanding the reality shock that always comes to make possible the advance in the search for truth, as we live in a universe that deliberately hides it, due to the way it was woven, but not finalized.

The claim may seem surprising, but even with new land and sea discoveries opening up this unique historical background, the repercussions of these achievements in academic circles are practically none. This implies a significant matter; historians are unaware of the history

---

[45] Dwarka "Sanskrit" means Gateway to heaven, discovered 36 m (120 ft) underwater in the Gulf of Cambay. It was found in the 19th century and should had existed around 32 million years ago.

that arises with the archaeological discoveries. And these have not really served any purpose, despite being there, challenging the usual short view of orthodoxy. For the blindness promoted by the moral corruption of researchers who kill the truth in the name of the funds and sponsorships they receive, it can never exist because it interferes with their interests.

When indications of the discovery of a new context exceed the necessary precautionary measure in any scientific search, this prudence must give way to a new Thesis to verify the scientific method's continuation. However, this is not quite what has happened with archaeological discoveries in general. Unspeakable interests are raised as defenders of prudence so that the new cannot replace the knowledge established by their conveniences.

As evident as it may be, the new truth no longer prevails by virtue of its indicatives or something else. Because the official voice that enthroned it turned silent for a long time, among the paths of corruption that sweeps the psyche of the Homo Sapiens species.

From this Indus Valley civilization, of an astonishing amount of 25,000 archaeological sites so far discovered there. Only 62 were explored until 2018. Of those that have already been studied somehow, the biggest and best known are Mohenjo Daro, Harappa, Ganweriwala, Rakhigarhi, Kalibangan, Dholavira, and the port city Lothal.

I emphasize that the ruins of the Indus valley were found by John and his brother Wiliam Brunton in 1856, who was responsible for constructing the East Indies railroad, and part of the ruins' bricks were used in this work. Only 6 years later, archaeological studies began, when the two large capitals – Mohenjo Daro and Harappa – were unearthed, in addition to Mehrgarh.

In these and other cities, Castes became the current organizational system that has guided those people's lives for millennia.

Dwarka, a port city, now submerged, had a suggestive meaning in its name – the name Dwaraka, in Sanskrit, means portal– since this port city was a gateway for foreigners into the Indian continent. Lord Krishna resided in it for a long time, although he also established himself in other places.

The ruins of the ancient city Dwarka were found under the sea after recent oceanographic studies near the modern temple city – Dwarka.

It should be noted that Dwarka is mentioned several times in the Mahabharata.

According to studious, this Indus Valley civilization, also known as Harappan or Dravidian culture, had its peak between 5,500 and 4,000 years B.C.E.

Other authors suggest that, in fact, the Indus Valley civilization, Summer and Babylon, formed a single civilization. The connection between them is indicated by seals found in these 3 regions.

It is also important to emphasize that there is no historical accuracy to define at which point in the heyday of some of these cities the Caste system was put in place. Because it is not considered a critical detail, and not all will accept it anyway.

This fact is known, but it has never been deepened by the studious, which never allowed a glimpse of what actually happened in those days; about the vision of Dharma, Varna ad Karma it will always be a question for some people.

After the aforementioned Pre-Vedic Era, the so-called Vedic Era began around 6,500 years B.C.E, which extended to about 4,500 years B.C.E.

It was there that the 4 Vedas[46] were produced, elaborated by the great Rishis (class of non-human beings) of the past, that inhabited the Indus valley, as well as the banks of the Saraswati river – always mentioned in these 4 Vedas.

Historians point out that the end of the Vedic Era was marked by the Mahabharata war, which studious plotted in the year 5,102 B.C.E, and that coincides with the beginning of Kali Yuga – a period of darkness and challenges referred to in the Puranas[47], Tantra[48] , and

---

[46] Vedas Krishna, divided the Vedas into four parts and taught them to four of his disciples.

[47] Puranas are a vast collection of Indian literature that cover a waide range of topics, such as legends and traditional folklore.

[48] Tantra is a method to expand the mind and liberate the dormant energy, scriptures refer to techiniques for achieving a result.

Sastras[49], considered as part of the literature known as Smriti[50], by Hindus.

Here, again, I force myself to emphasize that I'm not at all convinced that the times described in the Mahabharata correspond to the time stamp commonly mentioned by historians. As I said, from the information I have, those facts took place in even older times.

During this period, the Vedas, which had been recited for millennia, began to be written on banana leaves, and some interpretations of these recitations were also produced, also done by the Rishis, to more easily reach the common man.

More recently, the Brahmanic Era began, which lasted from 4,500 to 3,500 B.C.E. During this period, Vedic knowledge was reserved for Brahmins or the Caste of priests; from this historical landmark, the Caste system became an immutable political-religious reality for humans.

The formulas and hymns that the priests practiced during the rituals of that time contained – as they have today – explanations of myths and cosmogonic narratives and ancient legends. Which are historical vestiges of India's past and the Aryan expansion through the Indus Valley, promoting the famous Indo-European migration, so commented by certain historians.

---

[49] Sastras is generally used as a suffix in the Indian literature context.

[50] Smriti sacred literarure based on human memory.

There is, however, another group, composed of more recent historians, saying that the Aryan invasion never existed, as the Aryans were always Indians and inhabitants of the Indus Valley (like the Dravidians). However, there was, indeed, the Aryan migration, which brought with it a compendium of coexistence with beings of the Demo class, notably the Lords who form the Trimurti and their hierarchical descendants.

To better understand Caste' system and the belief that Hindus have about them, we must emphasize a certain aspect of their scriptures.

Those scriptures considered Smriti are secondary – because there are the Vedic Shruti scriptures, considered the main ones – and among these, we have.

- The Dharma Shastras, which are the books that codify the laws that regulate Society.
- The Itihasa, or the so-called national epics.
- The Puranas, which are seen as popular religious education books.
- The Agamas, about devotional tendencies.
- The Dharshanas present the leading school of thought born from the Vedas.

What is the main issue? The books that make up the Dharma Shastra are precisely the Caste regulations and obligations composed by the Brahmins.

At that time, it is necessary to reflect on another aspect that weighs on the Caste system, as we need to understand that these texts were written by the invading

Proto-Austrian (so-called by some historians) or Aryan people as a way of dominating Indian society.

The individuals of that Aryan people, again (in the sense of readjusting), fixed the Caste system, becoming the dominant Caste when they assumed Brahmins' role. However, not all Indian nuclei accepted the Vedic imposition of the Caste system, and a considerable part of society, which was not in agreement, took refuge in the forest, initiating a new body of religious literature from the Hindus, which are the Aranyakas texts, also known as the *Books of the Forests.*

In this way, the habit arose, among the Hindus, to isolate themselves in search of wisdom, and this came from a small group of initiates who departed to the silence of the forests in search of other ways of salvation and philosophical speculations.

These ascetics opposed the mechanics of complicated sacrifice rites and the appropriation, practiced by the Brahmins, of all knowledge and religious acts and rituals.

It was based on the time mark of the year 3,900 B.C.E that the Aranyakas and also the Upanishads emerged, the so-called literature of the Aranya (forest) tradition. In those times, there were vast and leafy forests located on the banks of the river Ganges.

The oldest of the Dharma Shastra is that of the mythical ancestor of the Manava tribe, called Manu.

10th Verification

Manu's laws brought even more benefits and powers to the Brahmin's Caste, and it makes strengthening its dominance over Indian society.

Note that the laws of Manu determined that the Brahmins owned everything in the universe and that they should not be charged taxes because an angry Brahmin could, just by reciting a mantra – sound or set of sounds that are an instrument of thoughts and which contain a specific power – destroy an entire army.

I cannot resist saying that the laws that Moses, under the domain of Yahweh, enacted for the twelve Hebrew tribes to educate their peers, even become nice compared to the laws of Manu.

Extreme?

Manu's laws were even stricter in penalties to the Sudras. If a Sudra abused a Brahmin woman. He would have his property confiscated and his sexual organ cut off. If a Seddra heard the recitation of the Vedic scriptures, the punishment was to receive the molten lead in their ears. If recited, he would have his tongue cut out, and so on. According to Manu's laws, women were considered a source of dishonor, discord and should be avoided, and married women should show devotion to their husbands.

Finally, the laws of Manu were a powerful instrument of social control and maintenance of the power of the Brahmins. According to what is known in Spirituality, it was because of those concepts that a specific genetic sequence emerged in a particular area of human DNA. That specific genetic sequence which would later be the basis of the Nazi behavior. However, human knowledge will never understand this assertion. The future will tell!

Thus, the Post-Vedic or Upanishadic Era emerged, which lasted from 3,500 to 3,000 B.C.E.

The term Upanishad derives from the Sanskrit words upa (near), ni (below), and shad (to sit), representing the act of sitting on the floor next to a spiritual master to receive instruction.

The WHO AM I? have its origin in Upanishads, as the highest point of the Vedas.

The knowledge of the Upanishads destroyed ignorance, the seed of Samsara –the reincarnation circuit.

They are responses to questions from very well-prepared disciples, in which what is transmitted only eliminates all ignorance and leads to liberation – or Moksha.

Around 3,000 to 2,100 B.C.E, the Pre-Classical or Epic Era takes place. In that era, the epics of Ramayana and Mahabharata were transferred from oral traditions to written records. Within a view to posterity enthroning the cultural traits and panels of both, notably in the Mahabharata, the validity of the Caste system. More recently, the Classical, Tantric, and Puranic Ages took place, all maintaining the Castes' functioning normality.

In this way, a woven system to educate Demo beings became a dire heritage for humanity, who received this historical legacy without ever realizing its real colors, because of the lens of religious faith, which only sees what is already determined by it to be the truth.

In this current era that we live in, we can observe how all the accumulated weight of so many holy scriptures – that considered the Caste system to be an existential program coming from gods – ended up definitively imposing itself on the suffering Hindu people.

It may seem foreign to Western thought, but it was in this way, through the bias of religiosity, that the Caste system came to weigh on the most modern human organizations on the Indian continent.

Honestly, I think that there would never be a Caste system to educate people to submit to their apparent destiny, without ever revolting, if the obligation to fulfill that fate had not been transformed into a sacred duty, and as being the will of gods – which seems disgusting to me.

What kind of gods would have such weird and unflattering wishes?

It seems to be a question that nobody asks, which makes everything even stranger.

I, therefore, undertake to do them!

11th Verification

We are sowing an absolutely mistaken and infantilized concept of gods, and this spread was the beginning of all humanitarian crimes. Along with the naive and unhappy human existence!

The curious thing is that this is seen as a blessing from gods for those gathered in Castes. The duty corresponding to each Caste should be considered the obligation of their lives.

How was this submission virus rooted in the human psyche? The obligation to perform – so strongly emphasized in the religious belief of the Hindus – was cultivated in such a way that the process of loyalty to the personal conscience was seen as a simple wave in the middle of the ocean surrounded by a collective belief. This faith, grounded as sacred in hearts infantilized by ignorance, turns into blindness concerning the natural philosophical justifications that would repudiate or, at least, would find it weird that the human being is transformed into a robot of Dharma.

That done, the confirmation bias pointed out by cognitive psychologists completes the work of feeding back the perennial process of domination of the strongest over the weakest, the most ancestral of the problems of this universe and Creation as a whole because born with the psychic reconstruction of the fallen Creator himself, which needs to survive at all costs and always be the strongest, to rule over everything else.

The genetic sequences that support this psychological premise make up the most emblematic markings in all existing species' genomes.

The perennial feeling of resignation, associated with that of mission accomplished, according to the precepts of the Dharma of each Caste, produces the hormonal game of the chemistry of the human brain that causes the satisfaction of serving gods, the exultation to live what gods decreed, and the feeling of being cared by gods becomes the greatest gifts to be received.

The curious and sad enigmatic aspect, present in a dominating way in the psyche of the species, is that this chain of psychic stages, which dressed Demo dementia like a jewel, also began to adorn the human psyche. However, they do not suffer from dementia – that, in humanity, is atavistic asleep in some regions of the so-called trash DNA, which accounts for about 95% to 97% of the genome of each human being.

However, if well awake, brainwashing, and conditioning techniques, this dementia returns to some degree to occupy the human psyche. It was – and it is – exactly what continues to be true among the ranks of this humanity that have directly received the weight of this demodharmic legacy, supported by the law of Dharma, of Demo culture.

12th Verification

The hormonal peace, felt by the human being who resigns and, thus, sees himself as fulfilling the gods' will. A gods that take care of him, who watches over his well-being, becomes the seal or the lock that guarantees the quality of the submission.

The Hindus even went so far as to exalt this submission through the joy of exaltation, called Ananda[51], which, at first, seems to be a human behavior worthy of an evolutionary score, when, in fact, it is not because it kills, in that same human being, his possibilities to wake up thousands of talents that the human genome holds – a very different aspect of the Demo genome, which only allows one to have very few talents, precisely because of dementia that is inevitable in them, which can only be reduced, but never completely overcome.

The Demo, now located and imprisoned again in their homes – or loka that is situated in the antimaterial world that is parallel to ours – they follow this process from there, exactly through the observation of this hormone soup that makes human beings feel happy even if they live in disgrace and cannot leave it because this is gods' will.

The Hindu way of thinking uses shattered apologies, enlightened or not, to justify what still happens there, as if it had a blessing from the past that, one day, was made possible in earthly culture.

Although modern Indian governments have officially eliminated the Varna-Caste factor from Hindu society, the weight of their tradition prevails, and, in practice, the breakdown continues as it has always been.

Unfortunately, we humans who, much later, orally inherit these mythological traditions – here I am not

---

[51] Ananda means bliss or happiness.

referring only to the issue of Varnas – we have never managed to break free from them.

The worst thing is that, when transcribing to paper, we call gods everything that was not human and, since then, the misuse of this concept has become the sacred and unchanging keynote of religious beliefs, which prevents serious and adult perception of the actual concept of gods, which, one day, we will still discover.

Through this practice that has become usual, we have become accustomed to transforming strange and even bestial beings into gods and, today, we cannot get rid of this burden because religious zeal does not allow it. There you go.

It is tremendously difficult for my sensitivity because of my understanding that Shiva, Krishna, and Sai Baba – the same being manifest in the different projection of energy, as I think, acting at different times, but with the same mark, adapted to the temporal factor – they defend Castes as a way of spiritual progress for individuals.

If coming from Shiva, I can still accept this behavior because he became part of the creation there were not even human beings. As for Krishna, I still conceive of a kind of understanding and acceptance for his stance in the same direction, also due to the circumstances of the time he lived, when existing human beings were still sort of intelligent pets. However, I cannot accept Sai Baba's position, despite understanding the Demo influence on his psyche and the fact that he again plunged into the old vein of the Hindu priestly lineage, all contaminated this and other matters arising from demonic culture. This contamination will be deeply addressed in The Forgotten Legacy. Yoga of the Trimurtians, another book written by me.

13th Verification

It is terrible to see how the misery of hundreds of millions of human beings, disciplined in Ahimsa, started to serve as means of spiritual readjustment when they are given no other option than only being able to evolve through acceptance of the facts.

It's better to try and fail than never to try at all, or It's better to try and fail than never know and always wonder, but due to ahimsa, **they can't even try!**

At first, it seems to be extremely beautiful, becomes ugly and criminal due to the use made of people's ingenuity and conditioning, condemned to subject themselves so horribly to false gods, even if they do it in good faith.

What kind of being could want or need this type of submission?

Let's face it; there is something very wrong with this proposition!

Thanking gods for starving, having no place to live, and other deprivations of every kind, again, let's face it. This is great for the Brahminic elite and different faces of the same power. Why would gods need this? Even more, why would gods need this to continue? Will it have to be this way as long as life in India exists?

Nowadays, it is immoral to defend a situation like that of the Castes, even if only out of fear of an uncontrollable demographic or social explosion.

The amazing thing is that they, Shiva and Brahma are responsible, spiritually and mentally speaking, whether for the first or the eleventh hour of this problem. Still, they live as if it were up to humans to solve all sorts of difficulties that they generated with their oddities – and the worst thing is that it seems that it has to be that way due to these beings' absolute incompetence resize what they did.

To think that this kind of problem is not even weighted by Spirituality is kind of disturbing for this old scribe who would instead do anything else than having the responsibility to address topics as hard as these, and the worst, lonely!

3. Beyond the Castes

The human way of existing has caused a change in the way the so-called scientific laws of this Creation have come to act in their quantum context, with consequences in the spiritual environments and in the two universes that characterize this Creation. (known as Brahmaloka[52] and Buhloka[53] in Sanskrit). That even the Spiritual Revelation that occurred in the second half of the 19th century could not explain, nor Sai Baba from the 20^{Th} to the 21st century could not explain the change.

This statement, which I register here, is the interpretation that I am obliged to make in the face of the facts I was able to discover. The emergence of human rationality in the condition in which it occurred marked codes on the electrons and genomes of this Creation.

The acute sense of the human, associated with human philosophical reasoning, is capable of valuing emotions with superior and refined standards. These standards established reduction on the untidy way in

---

[52] Brahmaloka is Brahma antimaterial universe parallel to our material universe where everything started with his DNA.

[53] Buhloka is our material universe.

which evil and ignorance had been acting freely in Creation, practiced by the demonic classes. The demonic classes have been created in the sad history of Brahmaloka – the universe that exists parallel to ours, the origin of the Angel-clone and Demo life.

In other words, the biological life that emerged in humans had a complexity. The Angel-clone and Demo life got mixed with the biological creation, then the Karma arising from the non-fulfillment of the Dharma with its positive and negative consequences was used both for the immortal spirits of the Demos and for the transient egos of biological beings.

It is good not to forget that according to the mythological news – which, by the way, were not fake news, even though they were considered like that by the academic arrogance – it was the Demon and biological kingdoms, the ones generating life with some or much complexity. That complexity continued producing new species or experiencing the final unfolding of previous genomes over the 13.8 billion years in which the two universes of this Creation exist.

In understanding Demodharmic culture, the more elaborated one, born much more recently in terms of universal time. The simple issue of whether or not to apply the Dharma criteria as a moral duty would define everything else. On the other hand, in the newly emerged human culture, more sophisticated and complex than the Demo kind. The absence of love and the inability to forgive have become essential aspects associated with the laws of cause and effect (action and reaction), which demanded higher and more refined standards of conduct for enlightened earthlings.

How important is that? Humans were led to think that they had gods, and divine justice, something that Demons never thought of before them. At the beginning of times for this Creation, there were already very evolved beings that determined how they should live. The dominant elite that was Trimurti, was completely unaware of this fact. Because they knew that, among the Demo generations, all of them disputed the power all the time through another – and that of the prevalence of the stronger over, the weaker. That was all!

Hard to understand? Perhaps. I know this aspect of the facts corresponds exactly to the opposite of what all religions have always claimed to be the truth.

The sad thing is that this compendium of high knowledge has remained hidden because the forces that dominated life on Earth have constantly mistreated the truth having it as the last flag to be waved in this world.

Perhaps, one of the most brilliant minds – observing from the scientific perspective – that has already walked among humans has been that of Albert Einstein. Possessed of intellectual lenses that allowed him to envision scenarios, contexts, and circumstances situated beyond common sense, Einstein was a scientist who did not stop at the final result pointed out by mathematics. In addition to being a master in the art of deciphering how things and processes happen – which is the real domain of science – his searching mind allowed him to surpass the apparent limit imposed by the scientific method and entered, with the same spirit of inquiry, into the field of why, which was restricted to philosophy, although constantly invaded by religion, which is already supposed to be the owner of the truth and the whys.

Modern scientists considered that Galileo, Kepler, Newton, as well as Einstein were brilliant minds. Still, they could not free themselves from that first cause as it was particularly impossible not to revere it when they lived, even though dangerously mixing metaphysics, colored by religion, with cold science, which allows putting chance as the primary cause. This, let's face it, leaves the principle of everything colorless and is filled with even more weird explanations than the existence of a Creative Mind located beyond human comprehension.

Suppose nothing is known about the principle of the causes that turned the wheel of this Creation and its machine to produce life. It is an arduous mission to find the appearance of the human being.

Let's complicate it further, discovering whether the mind or, to put it another way, whether consciousness is part of nature or not seems to be another arduous task. Unresolved until today, no matter how much authorities on the subject allow themselves to pontificate about it.

Deepak Chopra and Menas Kafatos, in the book *You Are the Universe*, offer a very interesting reflection on the issues above, notably because they do so from a conversation between two brilliant minds at the time of the 1930s, which I will reproduce from page 21 to 25.

Because Einstein is almost the symbol of a staggeringly great mind, most people don't realize that after the great triumph of General Relativity, which took place when he was just in his mid-thirties, Einstein bet on the wrong side of modern physics because he couldn't accept its conclusions. When he famously said that he didn't believe that God played dice with the universe, Einstein stated his opposition to the uncertainty and randomness of quantum behavior. He placed his lifelong faith in a unified creation that operated without rifts, tears, and separations.

The notion that there is one reality and not two was something Einstein strove to prove until his death in 1955, but this quest was so far from the mainstream of physics that he was considered an incidental thinker after the 1930s – in their franker moments, even his greatest admires shook their heads over such a great mind spending decades chasing a will-o'-the-wisp. But on one occasion, he was given a clue about how to escape the trap posed by relativity and quantum mechanics. The escape route wasn't scientific, however, but came from a poet.

On July 14th, 1930, reporters from around the world gathered outside Einstein's house in Caputh, an outlying village in Berlin favored by the well-to-do as an escape from the hustle and bustle of the city. The occasion was a visit by Rabindranath Tagore, a great Indian poet than at the height of his fame. Born to a prominent Bengali family in 1861, almost twenty years before Einstein, Tagore had lept into the Western imagination by winning the Nobel Prize for Literature in 1913. He was also a philosopher and musician, someone the West viewed as an embodiment of Indian spiritual traditions. The purpose of Tagore's visit with "the world's greatest scientist," as Einstein was popular – and probably rightly – known, was to discuss the nature of reality.

As science raised serious doubts about the religious worldview, readers felt that Tagore enjoyed an uncanny and very personal connection with a higher world. Reading even a few snippets of his writings creates the same impression today.

I feel this pang inside –
Is it my soul trying to break out,
Or the world's soul trying to break in?
My mind trembles with the shimmering leaves.
My heart sings with the touch of sunlight.
My life is glad to be floating with all things
Into the blue of space and the dark of time.

On that July day, as their conversation was recorded for posterity, Einstein was more than politely curious about Tagore's worldview – he recognized the appeal of an alternative reality.

Einstein asked the first question. "Do you believe in the Divine as isolated from the world?"

Tagore's reply, delivered in flowery Indian English, was a surprise. "Not isolated. The infinite personality of Man comprehends the universe. There cannot be anything that the human personality cannot subsume… the truth of the Universe is human truth."

Tagore then set out a theme that blended science and mysticism into a metaphor. "Matter is composed of protons and electrons… The entire universe is linked up with us, as individuals, in a similar manner – it is a human universe."

In a simple phrase – the human universe – Tagore had posed the ultimate challenge to materialism. He had also undermined the cherished belief in a divine universe. Materialism would place human beings as an accidental creation that occurred on a speck of a planet awash in billions of galaxies. Religion, in its most literal interpretation, would place God's mind infinitely beyond the human mind. Tagore believed neither o these things, and Einstein immediately becomes engaged, as the transcript shows.

Einstein: There are two different conceptions about the nature of the universe - the world as a unit dependent on humanity and the world as a reality of the human factor.

Tagore renounced this either/or proposition.

Tagore: When our universe is in harmony with man, the eternal, we know is as truth, we feel is as beauty.

Einstein: This is the purely human conception of the universe.

Tagore: There can be no other conception.

He wasn't spouting poetic fancy or even mystical dogma. Tagore – flowing robes and sage's long white beard notwithstanding – for seventy years had been coming to terms with the scientific view of reality, and he felt that he could counter it with something deeper and closer to the truth.

Tagore: This world is a human world… the world apart from us does not exist. It is a relative world, depending for its reality upon our consciousness.

No doubt Einstein understood the implications of Tagore's "human universe, " and he didn't ridicule it or attempt to undermine it. But he couldn't accept it, either. The most pointed exchange immediately followed.

Einstein: Truth, then, or the beauty is not independent of man?

Tagore: No.

Einstein: If there would be no human beings anymore, the Apollo Belvedere (a famous classical statue in the Vatican) would no longer be beautiful.

Tagore: No.

Einstein: I agree with regard to this conception of beauty, but not with respect to truth.

Tagore: Why not? Truth is realized through man.

Einstein: I cannot prove that my concept is right, but that is my religion.

It was astonishingly modest for Einstein to say that he couldn't prove that truth is independent of human beings, which is, of course, the cornerstone of objective science. Humans beings don't have to exist for water to be H2O or for gravity to attract interstellar dust and form stars. "I have faith that the objective world is real, even though I can't prove it."

This once-famous meeting between two great minds is now largely forgotten. But startlingly, it was prophetic because the possibility of a human universe, one that depends upon us for its very existence, now looms large. The most fantastic of possibilities that we are the creators of reality is no longer fantastic. After all, belief and disbelief are human creations, too.

14th Verification

By stating that God did not play dice, in addition to being mistaken in his metaphysical glimpse, he linked science to a type of cause that modern scientists do not often use.

I know that I am one voice alone in this type of approach about the reality in which we live, placing it as sick and full of wounds. In addition to pointing out the Creator as also sick, which, obviously, no thinker or scientist of today or in human history dared to formulate in the terms I presented the issue in some of my books and please find it in English in my book, *The Cosmic Drama of Yahweh* in Amazon.

On the academic side, I do not expect understanding or acceptance of this thesis, not even as a possibility of study.

In any case, the previous condition of the fallen being who came to present himself as Brahma/Yahweh was problematically planned and later manipulated by more than one mind – as the mythological reports demonstrate, notably the Aryan / Hindu. Making things even worse, this range of reality in which we live could never be finished because of Brahma's problem at the beginning of the creation. Everyone who appears in it suffers from its same problems and cannot decipher it, much less readjust it and transcend it. What to do?

No scientist said it, but Einstein's phrase God does not play dice with the universe was expressed by him because there was an assumption that God was perfect and therefore, he could not play dice to see what result it would get since, being God, the creative process could not be like that.

The uncertainty about the location of certain fundamental portions of matter (protons, neutrons, electrons, and photons), if they would work as a wave or even as a particle, among other aspects, which would be understood – as I tried to address in the book "The Cosmic Drama of Yahweh," Portuguese version published in 2010 – as one of the effects of a problematic Creation, whose Author could not be perfect. However, this would be unbearable for the academic world, which criticizes Einstein's romantic notion of a deistic God behind

Creation (as well as the notion of the watchmaker who produces a watch and leaves it), let alone he would do so in the face of the idea, not of a perfect God, but a complicated and problematic Being-Creator.

There will never be an escape route to the apparently elegant way in which science usually finds explanations about the principle of everything – even more difficult to verify than the notion of randomness, that of a perfect God, or even that of a Being-Creator/Trimurti who made a mistake in generating this range of reality and the life that arose from it – as avatars, saints, prophets and sociologists usually excuse themselves for maintaining the Caste system in India, due to the Dharma of a collectivity.

Even being the formulator of the most brilliant ideas of humankind, Einstein always misinterpreted the larger context about a universe that he thought was static, but that, in fact, was expanding, as well as that God didn't throw dice to generate the universe, even though the calculations of quantum mathematics and cosmology pointed exactly to that or something even more disturbing behind Creation.

Why am I linking scientific issues and the concept of gods to the case of Hindu Castes? Because humanity needs to review, urgently, the concept it has built about gods so that it is not used criminally and mistakenly, as certain religions have done. Unfortunately, this was practiced in inquisitive Catholicism. At the same time,

Islam continues to issue Fatwa[54]– religious decisions expressed by muftis, considered Islamic academic authorities – in the name of Allah, which implies the death of infidels. Hinduism cages hundreds of millions of people in an unworthy way of life, for that is God's will and, therefore, the sacred duty of living life this way has to be fulfilled under penalty of being punished, even more, contracting negative karma. Now, let's face it: it all has to stop!

Humanity needs to get out of this permanent stage of spiritual infantilism to that of adulthood. However, how can we take this path with this type of belief in gods who order the killing of people and who change his mind over time, currently considering as unfaithful who, in the past, was part of his then elected people?

After all, what gods are these? What universe is this? What kind of life is this? What religions are these? What human being is this who submits to these oddities, and all sorts of crimes against oneself and the life one manages to dispose of?

What science still cannot see, it seems that, effectively, only the eyes of poetry or those not concerned with academic lenses can glimpse.

In the human condition, Tagore saw in the nature of each of us an infinite pattern of personalities capable of co-creation and even defining values for the contours of

[54] Fatwa is a nonbinding legal opinion on a point of Islamic law given by a qualified jurist in response to a question.

the truth surrounding us and which we are a part of. He saw far when he realized that the universe was becoming humanized, which gives me the strength to defend the thesis that the Creator himself is also in the process of humanization, assimilating the donations of the genetic memories that earthlings are producing, even if unconsciously.

However, even being human, we need to humanize ourselves even more, definitively separating ourselves from the Demo infection present in our inherited DNA. Due to the fact that this DNA has already arrived here on Earth, about 3.8 billion years ago, with its cancer marks and atavistically selfish – exactly how, today, the genetic autopsy manages to read these facts – its codified features need to be readjusted, reordered by the spiritual evolution of the increasingly humanized and spiritualized beings.

Let there be many apparent pleonasms aiming to draw the attention of my contemporaries to how shameful it is for us to continue to be so little of what we could be. If we opted for the superior conduct of the supreme values of existence that, even in the midst of the ocean of ignorance in which we were forced to emerge for life, we managed to build and distinguish in the field of decency of noble principles and purposes.

We still need to experience them even more, and there is no way to do so by living with the many Caste systems on their local faces, sadly nationalized in many quarters of the planet in the form of diverse ghettos, based on racism, a mark of those who are more for the cretinous than for the humanization of the planetary family.

May future generations pay attention to what I wanted to convey here, even though I know that the smallness that characterizes my human condition would almost completely destroy the attempt to address such a complex topic! However, I am doing it!

There is much more to be perceived beyond the Castes, especially regarding the "used to it," "resigned" way of behaving, as the Human Spirit – believe it, it exists, and it's all of us – has dealt with this and other themes of the calamitous ancestral heritage that hangs over our shoulders, degrading what remains of the consciousness of our species.

Although apparently, the present attempt is presented as being destroyed by my own incompetence, I was not defeated by the fear of failing so bad in the face of this unusual subject, that being the only payment I take for the boldness, which satisfies me spiritually, and that is enough for me.

May the humanism of the adult people (today we prefer our spiritual child vision) who will one day walk on this planet effectively dignify human existence, and well above the weirdness of the outdated and anachronistic theologies that victimize the progress of the earthlings, leading them to think that they are sinners mistakenly, children of the devil, spiritual traitors, that is, defective since their genesis.

Well, if there is a defect in our genes, it's not our fault, for we didn't do it!

May future generations realized that, despite the problems that we have in our Human nature, we are, yes, part of the heroes who carry on their shoulders the weight of the iniquity of a Creation that should never have existed!

4. The Forgotten Demonic Culture

The antimaterial universe and the material universe were created. Extraterrestrial groups of physical beings and beings without physical form that in the future would be known as the families of the Demos resided on Earth with human ancestors. Those beings claimed to be gods.

They took advantage of the naivete of our ancestors. Just as the same way we currently do with the innocence of some of the species of terrestrial nature, which we train and feed on.

During millennia before the flood, the Nephilim, biological beings mentioned in the Bible and the Demo being (extra physical beings considered as gods in Greek and Hindu mythology); they developed and collected a set of information that has been kept away from the curiosity of our ancestors so that it could be considered sacred.

In figure 1, we see that in our evolution, we emerged as Homo Sapiens that had lived more closely with those beings as Zeus from the Olympus and Anunnaki or Nephilim, in Sumerian. Those beings were considered gods and significantly interfered in the development of the Homo Sapiens species over the millennia - there are other human species with different degrees of consciousness inhabiting different worlds of this biological universe.

The expression gods had a distorted view that still currently marking and continues to be part of human logic. These gods were poorly understood, so they were thrown into Greek mythology, where everything that is incomprehensible there seems to fit well. Most of us can admit the mystery behind the concept. We generalize our understanding of these gods as beings from outside.

I say from the outside because one should not understand it only as extraterrestrial beings belonging to any world of this material universe. In addition to this component, another already mentioned above points to beings of a Demo genus, citizens of worlds located in other dimensions, who seem to have had an open connection with Earth in the past and, more broadly, with our range of this universal reality.

Various mythologies confuse those trying to understand the multiple narratives of beings who came over using ships and others who flew without artifacts. Some of them modified their bodies in front of others' eyes and were apparently deformed, showing mental powers. In contrast, others, deprived of these faculties of the mind, presented only the technological equipment they had.

In many respected research papers had a similarity between Enlil and Zeus. But Enlil is a being who came from another world with biological life; he was an Anunnaki (Akkadian) or Nephilim (Sumerian) astronaut on a mission on Earth. At the same time, Zeus is a demonized being who was born or, better saying, created on Earth within a Demo family. Whose members resided in an astral/celestial abode called Olympus and could move from it to our planetary stage. So, let's face it, these are very different situations. However, they are different beings; even dough, many think they are the same character because it's wrongly pointed out by excellent studious of the subject.

Despite the respect I have for the authors and, in particular, for the magnificent works – such as the books written by Zecharia Sitchin[55] – that give support for some of the conclusions of the subjects studied. I think it is very prudent that we do not close this issue, as it has yet to be assessed in terms of the magnitude of all its elements. Some of which have never been considered until now, weakening the definitive assertions on a subject that still needs to be better appreciated by future human generations.

Some authors drew a parallel between Yahweh and Enlil, Enlil and Zeus, Enki and Prometheus, Enki and Lucifer, Zeus and Odin. But for my channeling work and direct contact with these beings. I am being forced to reveal the results of my experiences, and I want to leave it clear that I may be correct or mistaken.

---

[55] Zecharia Sitchin attributed the creation of the ancient Sumarian culture to the Anunnaki, a race of extraterrestrial from a planet beyond Neptune called Niburi.

It is not the goal in this book to evaluate which of the mythologies can be compared. For example, that Zeus was the same Aryan/Hindu god called Indra. The Greek and Hindu stories corresponded to the same characters, despite the peculiarities of each of them. However, from what I was able to perceive and the facts that I am obliged to experience. These two mythological currents do have something in common that makes them unique. Both describe occurrences related mainly to demonized beings and their technological power in a time when they thought they would definitely settle on Earth and dominate it for posterity.

The Sumerian mythology, on the other hand, practically in all its entirety, refers to extraterrestrial beings who landed here using their ships - as so well decoded by Zecharia Sitchin in his works, among other authors and studious who, in the nineteenth century, started to decipher Sumerian writing. Since then, they have already pointed out this possibility. However, there is no pure mythology concerning this apparent dichotomy (beings from outside = extraterrestrials + extra physical) because none of them was written just in the exact single moment, in the same historical period, which always led to the addition of future narratives, according to the knowledge of the times. This aspect, among others, completely disfigured certain Summaries due to the mixture of situations and contexts that, in fact, were separated.

Advanced studious defend the thesis that there was only one extraterrestrial civilization at work here. They researched to understand the similarity between gods of all mythologies, which cannot be done satisfactorily.

For example, Egyptian mythology seems to have assimilated the two components more strongly than the others – the extraterrestrial and extra physical contexts, although they occurred at different times and were treated as one. I mention these facts just to reason why it is dangerous to conclude the pages of an era in which the panorama still needs to be prudently and boldly unveiled.

Finally, I invite you not to give as sure or truth as what the human species still have to discover.

This implies reaffirming that these book pages should only be seen as another modest attempt to unveil what covers the mythological bias. Many seekers of the truth whose lenses are still polluted by exacerbated scientism or gods-producing faith make everything that comes from the ancestral past transformed into a religion.

Everything that I tried to reflect on these pages, for those who read them, is just a new premise before what we have faced as the truth about the past.

I refer to a culture arising from the knowledge of these two civilizing focuses of the past. The legacies of extraterrestrial beings and the nonphysical beings, whose fragments reached up to modern times under the aforementioned mythological bias. The mythology which is present in our psyche. We were conditioned to consider this whole collection of facts as being untruths. Our ancestor cleverly put together for different purposes.

In my studies, I have called the nonphysical, cultural component Demodharmic because it belongs to the Demo culture, and it's linked to the concept of Dharma.

Bizarrely, even singular figures – such as Sai Baba – supported or justified the Castes' existence, which seems to me to be a spiritual contradiction, hard to explain, but I will not escape from this analysis.

In the eyes of Hindus – and those who have eyes in the western and eastern can see the significance of the Trimurti's avatars and their missions on Earth – Sai Baba is an avatar of Shiva, and I think he was created in the manner of Krishna, that is, with the same level of consciousness that was behind Lord Krishna, who was another avatar of Shiva, conceived in ancient times.

Regarding this issue, there are still controversies of all kinds among Krishna's followers, who regard him as Vishnu's avatar – but it does not matter much to our approach.

I defend the thesis that what solves this issue that divides the followers of Vishnu on the one hand and the followers of Shiva on the other, is the fact that Krishna is a Keshava avatar, that means generated from the mixed code of life of the 3 Lords of Trimurti – namely, Brahma, Vishnu and Shiva, the Trimurtian Gods.

Hindus have become used to the formatted system of their beliefs and have lived in it for millennia. Similarly, other countries have also become used to the moral and material disgrace that keeps the rich and the poor increasingly distant in terms of the material perspective. In the moral aspect, I have to ask myself if anything really separates us as members of a single planetary family?

The dimension of human drama seen in India's present days can only be found in religious fanaticism and, paradoxically. In the beauty of what this fundamentalist feeling produces in the resignation field.

Beauty? For many, yes! Because it keeps life flowing in the miserable conditions in which many Hindus find themselves, and even so, without major upheavals and altercations. If things are like that because it is the will of a god, what will a Hindu do if he believes that this is his Karma?

Why the paradox? Because beautiful concepts like Ahimsa – which means avoidance of violence in any form of expression, whether oral or attitudinal – have been transformed into controlling tools or were born as if they could give some kind of genetic support to the genome of those who would, later on, come to compose the Castes, as we are seeing here.

15th Verification

Either it was in the name of progress, or someone simply took advantage of the beautiful concept of Ahimsa. To condition individuals to acquire or appropriate certain postures of personal contrition, the only way to educate the arrogant, reluctant, and hardened personalities in execrable behaviors.

Studying India and the wonderful conception of its philosophical assumptions, I had the impression that the soul of the world was there, in its amazing priestly lineage formed by very special beings who, since legendary immemorial times, kept the light of several clarifications on for people's progress.

Things are this way because Lord Shiva, through his avatars, established a continuous process of teaching and enlightenment for those who lived on Earth, and, in the beginning, they were non-human creatures, although rationalized to a certain degree. They came to be considered gods by the humans who emerged in the midst of it. However, because they emerged as members of the Homo genus during this context, the so-called humans inherited the teachings conveyed by these non-human beings to their peers, who then lived on this planet that we now call ours.

Many misunderstandings began to be collected from this coexistence of different genus in the emerging human culture and psych.

The first misunderstanding was to confuse this nonphysical dimension or this parallel universe with the spiritual reality, which lies beyond these two universal sections of this improper creation – which arose from the singularity that, through the Big Bang, theory initiated not only this universal dimension which we live in but also the demonic dimension.

The other major misunderstanding, among many, was the aforementioned psychological conditioning of calling gods whatever was not human.

The so-called gods passed on to humanity the new legacy in which they were important and humans irrelevant, just as today, in human culture, we are superior, and we consider other animals to be far less important than us, or even of no importance.

16th Verification

The humans originated from Homo Sapiens. They ended up inheriting a life operating system that was created for Demo beings. The Demos dominated the earth, but humans ended up being the heirs of the planetary legacy.

When I realized that all of my joy in seeing something special – a spiritual pattern of superior conduct, of the Ahimsa. – happening nowadays. I faced the mistaken concept of Castes defended by a soul the size of Sai Baba's, and then I was forced to live with some beings that I'd always considered mythological. The foundation of my understandings, built until then, collapsed.

Due to the fact I lived with them, I had to open my eyes for what had become evident, and that's why this and some other books of my own were produced. To mention the misconception of the Caste system among terrestrial humans. This truth was established on Earth by beings who have always considered themselves the owners of truths revealed to humans. The no less disturbing aspect of always – in these avatars' forms, such as Rama, Krishna, Shankara, Jesus, Sai Baba, among others – presents themselves as agents of this process.

The misunderstanding is subtle but profound and disturbing.

Subtle because it rests in the confusion that the modern interpretation of the Hindu past facts produces while taking beings of demonic temper for human beings, in reading Hindu classics such as Ramayana and Mahabharata.

Profound because it has made miserable the way of life of billions of people – these avatars, however, claim that what they did has been and still is positive, since the human situation could be much worse – who have passed through this world, fanatic in demonic-temperament beliefs, in which mental power has been confused as being the spiritual power of the true gods that lies beyond the issues of Brahma, Vishnu, and Shiva, in the geopolitics of the Trimurti.

Disconcerting because these Lords of Trimurti think of themselves as gods, and their avatar's forms do it too, but in fact, they are not. However, their philosophical legacies, such as those of Krishna, Jesus, and Sai Baba, are the most beautiful side of what the religious feeling linked to its respective philosophical compendium, managed to produce and sow on Earth.

First, the Caste system's implantation occurred when the Demo Homo beings – classes of hybrid beings, with Demo and Homo genus – lived on Earth, and, later, it happened when humans were alone and inherited the entire tradition of this culture Demo Homo.

Despite the beauty I find in the Bhagavad Gita, in the gospels of Jesus' followers, and in the teachings of Sai Baba, I continue to search for the soul of the world, being free from the virus of the Demo temper – which I think I know exists in everything that the human forms (the avatars) of these beings made.

17th Verification

All of these avatars, due to the issue of the Demo genus stamped in their minds. They were susceptible and surrendered to Lila's every need. This always prevented them from seeing the universal reality when they were in a human form here.

One of the most painful aspects of this panorama, that involved the slow human progress. These avatars always left in the background the philosophical virtue of what they taught the humans insofar as they subordinated their strategies to the intended ends.

It was terrible for this writer to notice such a thing!

With this incongruity stamped on their faces and in their legacies, they demonstrated that they had the diploma of the old Demo incompetence of intending to teach what they could not practice themselves.

The Castes issue is just one of the disturbing aspects of this sad legacy.

5. Human Culture. Misunderstood Legacy

It's really not easy to break with the conditioning imposed by today's world. We have to take a free look at the way we live today. The terrestrial past and its influence on the way we live and the problems we have collected as cosmic species. We have been accustomed to finding the life we know as a godsend, which we should be grateful for.

Much more than these few millennia of years that humans/Homo Sapiens were here. Other races of beings, physical and not so physical, animalized and not so animal as we are, they had been here for many thousands of years before – had been feeling like the owners of Earth – they resided here, considering themselves the owners of this planet. Realizing this is an essential condition so that the enlightened understanding around the issue can be established in the human psyche.

The most widespread of all cultural legacies that arose even before the existence of the rational human being, and which ended up being passed on to its domain, was what, in this book, I called the Demo culture – in the present view, confused with mythology and not a reality. Even though it is strange to the elements that the flow of terrible events ended up making available to current generations of humans, it ended up being the great misfortune that blinded us to the point of taking a lie as truth. The lie that we have been alone on Earth all this time, and that is why we are owners of the planet.

This mythological legacy – the Demo culture – was passed on to humans and when the inevitable transition between news coming from oral traditions to the context of written material took place. It is also important for the reader to understand that, in some cultures, this transition was also made by beings who were not entirely human. In contrast, in other cultures, it was indeed done by the men and women of the ancient past.

Here, there is a however that needs to be registered when humans made the transition. As previously mentioned, many of the protagonists of the ancient oral versions, translated into human language. They were considered human beings when they had never been. Until today, they are thus described in many pages of mythological legends, so considered by current knowledge.

It had happened because non-human beings were the ones who registered, in writing, the ancient oral traditions., they did it so correctly, making the non-human characteristic of many of the ancient-tale beings clear. There were few situations in which this happened, but although they were rare, they were remarkable, as in the case of Jainism[56] and some of its unfolding.

Later and more widely, however, humans transferred the ancient ancestral knowledge, almost all registered in oral traditions, and later to the alphabets[57] that emerged. At that point in history, the problem of distortion arose in a drastic way because several protagonists were considered human, which disfigured the real plot.

Complicating the issue even more, the modern thought, illuminist, and post-illuminist forced themself to translate as being also human, the different beings found in the traditions of humanity's first forms of writing.

Thus, many of the tales currently considered Christian but were mythological – which is Beowulf's case, from the Nordic mythology – were Christianized, as if the characters were Catholic.

In this way, modern human culture is constantly being established on the ancient past with its mistaken values. And these misconceptions will possibly continue to pollute the minds of future generations. Permanently reminding them that we live under the constant weight of the worst type of dictatorship, cretinism is dressed up as an imposing religion.

---

[56] Jainism there are no gods or spiritual being. The 3 jewels are right belief, right knowledge and right conduct. The supreme principle is non violence (Ahimsa).

[57] Alphabets emerged 8th century B.themC. The Phoenician alphabet had spread to Greece.

We were never able to free ourselves from a control imposed in the ancient time there. But which remains acting on modern ideas and ideals, imposing its shadow, making the absence of clarification guarantee servitude.

It is sad to see a planetary civilization whose culture is based on deteriorated and mistaken stones. And its agents do not allow the simplest modification of any of its patterns.

In the realm of terrestrial culture, the ancient Hindu culture's particularities remain as weapons engaged to anyone who is trying to make a revolution in the face of what is entrenched in its roots.

Castes, racism, ghettos, refugee camps, homeless ethnicities, religious and political persecutions, patrolled by ideologies, and other oddities flood this crazy little world in which we live, debasing it, and we have no way of modifying the most basic standards of its organizational model, which obliges us to live with the slavery of everyone around these inheritances, until now apparently insurmountable.

Lost links maintain these ghostly shackles on this humanity's social and political relations, even though other types of beings were responsible for the behavioral genesis based on these vexing criteria.

According to the human model, the Castes represent nothing more than a mere copy of how demonic culture educated their peers, based on the concept of Dharma, which terms ended up involving the sad destiny of humanity.

18th Verification

This is the main aspect of the missing link—the misunderstanding around Demonic concepts, which had come to be seen and considered as human.

The look into the past shows that the human being who considers themselves modern needs to start from free of pre-conceived concepts. So that a new context can emerge. Unfortunately, at this point in the dramatically accumulated problem, I think that the lens of that look will never be able to see the size of the drama experienced by human and non-human ancestors in ancient immemorial times.

Perhaps, the current generation of men and women will never see the importance that human culture has to be productive for deciphering these conditions.

We have been programmed to think that we exist. But in fact, the genetic code of life that moves us is what lives in each tool-creature and belongs to intelligence that has gone sick. Therefore, it needs to use others too. Through them (his creation), he will see himself and realize what he did one day. However, at least for now, to perceive this prominent aspect of the issue would be frightening to many, besides seeming to be an apparent contradiction, hurting the common sense of our logic.

As mentioned, however, Maurice Maeterlinck, in her book. *The Life of the Bee*. Nobel Prize in Literature,

"Bees don't know if they will eat the honey they collect. We also ignore who will take advantage of the spiritual power that we introduce into the universe. In the same way that bees go from flower to flower, collecting more honey than they need for themselves and they're young, let us also seek, in reality, everything that can feed this incomprehensible flame in order to be willing to face any event with the security of the organic duty accomplished. Let us feed it with our feelings, with our passions, with everything we see, feel, hear, touch – and also with the very essence of it, which is the idea that can be deduced from discoveries, experiences, and observations made based on everything that is visited. Then comes a moment when everything turns so naturally into good, for a spirit that has submitted to the goodwill of truly human duty, that the very suspicion that the efforts you make may have no purpose makes it even more clear, purer, more disinterested, more penetrating and nobler the ardor of its investigations."

Indeed, it is difficult for human beings to perceive that their actions have to do with the notion, for the moment poorly understood, of the *Divine Favor*[58] , another book that I wrote, addressing the burden our spirits and their egos assume to exist for this Creation.

Perhaps, being unaware of this aspect of existence, Maeterlinck[59] usually says that.

---

[58] Divine Favor another Val Ellam' s only in portuguese for now.

[59] Maeterlinck was a Belgian playwright, poet, and essayist who was Flemish but wrote in French.

Intelligence is the faculty with the help of which we finally understand that everything is incomprehensible.

However, time will come when those issues that were hidden, lost, and therefore difficult to understand will be seen with the proper lenses and then will naturally reveal themselves to human logic.

Until then, however, ignorance and conditioning will cost a terrible price!

6. Totalitarian Genetics

Since the advent of human culture, the outside gods created a routine to establish a domination strategy. This strategy consisted of the system of choosing people on earth so that through this population, it can dominate the other nations.

One of these outside gods introducing himself as Brahma, to the Aryans and Hindus, he was known as Chaos, to the ancient Greeks, Ra-Atom, to the Egyptians, Yahweh, to the Jews and part of the West, Og-mi, to ancestral Celts, and Allah, to Muslims, among others, the fallen and demented Creator applied, until 2015, this criminal and inconsequential strategy of trying to dominate, at any cost, humans – who left its genetic control since the days of Pandora[60] as I tried to describe in another book called *Pandora's Smile*[61]. I classify this strategy this way from my perspective of human logic and

[60] Pandora was the first mortal woman in Greek mythology, a sort of Ancient Greek Eve. Zeus gave instruction to Hephaestus and all the other Olympina gods to create her for his revance.

[61] Pandora's Smile another Val Ellam's book that can be found in English at Amazon and throught the site https://pandoraunlock.com.

ethics. But for the outside gods – as they claim – the domination had always been the only way to be pursued, with the possibility of solving the Creator's old problem.

Since Pandora's event, when they lost control over humans. The question of how to regain the power to rule over the terrestrial human species and at the same time use them as a maneuver mass. They always wanted to use humans as a way to resolve the geopolitical disputes of the gods. The gods eventually had to get used and adapt to the growing advance of the dominated humans on Earth – which has always been seen as a place that belonged to the humans.

The Aryan, Jewish and Arab people were the 3 ethnic segments chose, with their own genetics – time will come when geneticists will understand, by the scientific method, what is being superficially stated here – that they were directly taken by the Creator Brahma to serve as the stage and, at the same time, an earthly army of his intentions.

Indirectly, the cultural trait of the Chosen People was later passed on by oral and also written tradition to many other people that would only appear later on. This was the case of the Hebrew tribes of the time of Heber, a descendant of Noah.

Who would evolve, many millennia later, to the two tribes of Judah, which one of them gave rise to the Jews? In continuation of the Jews' sequence on this concept of the Chosen People for their culture - as it's also the case with what was registered in Hindu mythology, built on the union of ancestral Aryan and Dravidian cultures.

Regardless of the angle one observes, this issue of exclusivity of the Chosen People had its origin in the organizational criteria of the Aryan Castes. Today called Hindu, which has always been used to refine certain areas of the Demo Homo genome, even though the terrestrial guinea pigs had never known, due to the absolute absence of knowledge and critical sense for that purpose – and the worst is that humanity still doesn't know about these facts at the beginning of the 21st century.

The Demo culture, especially that applied by the members of Trimurti, has always acted intending to create a Super-Segment among the people that inhabited the Earth. A handpicked the Chosen People so that it could fulfill the aims of the Creator. He would simply choose a given segment of humanity at a particular stage in history, then discarded them, and he would choose another, never worrying about what the feeling of exclusivity of the election, which he criminally conditioned the unsuspecting humans with, could provoke in terms of wars between people who considered themselves the Chosen People by the same Being that they had as a God.

If well observed, the historically structured hate between Arabs and Jews has to do with this sad aspect of the issue. As well as any trait of exclusivity and ethnic superiority that a people may feel had and has as its sickly basis, exactly the perspective that the stronger must always be imperial over the weaker.

Where did this perspective come from? This is one of the most detestable traits of the criminal and sick face of the Creator and which, unfortunately, is present in the genetic psyche of all species of living beings of terrestrial nature (to say the least), unfolded from its defining source code (known as DNA). These members of all species seek to survive at any cost, even if through killing so many others as if this behavior could have emerged as an inheritance from a Creator worthy of being called so.

With today's knowledge, an entity with these characteristics shouldn't be called God by any sensible person. However, this Being is still considered to be a God by more than 3 billion human beings.

Sancta simplicitas[62]!

For this afflicted writer, the most amazing thing was to realize that the so-called eugenics[63], established in the process of genetic manipulation to improve the race, is a trait that was born with the issue of Castes. And the worst, the disease of Nazism, among others, was established from the feeling of exclusivity that some German citizens of the late 19th and early 20th centuries felt. When in their eyes, it was finally time for the Aryan race to regain control of

---

[62] Sancta simplicitas! "O holy simplicity! In Latin is both to be innocent, humble and modest.

[63] Eugenics advocated selective breeding to achieve improving the genetic composition of the human race. Today we have technologies that make it possible.

the planet's destiny, after the blatant failures of the Jewish people (Judaism) and the Arabs (Islam). As already said.

Brahma / Yahweh / Allah, or whatever name we may use, must one day apologize to humanity for the number of crimes that its mental illness has imposed on the members of the earthly human family.

Trimurti's universal mismanagement is such that this problematic practice of the Chosen People was not only sown among earthly human beings – remember the reader that we humans are the last ones to have appeared within the scope of this universe. Therefore, we are the youngest race of all since, in a rational perspective, we have existed for about 50 thousand years – and this mismanagement has been occurring since the beginning of universal Creation, about 13.8 billion years ago. This implies that the 3 Lords had already made other Chosen People of Trimurti throughout this time, their weight had fallen on different species of both Demo kind – inhabitants of lokas or genus, in short, of the addresses that make up the antimaterial universe, parallel to ours – as biological kind, common to the species of the universe we live in.

In this way, these beings who have long been present on Earth have always disputed the issues of Lila – a game of power between the 3 Trimurti deities - and when humans emerged, the ancient disputes were passed on to human culture. In this transfer, however, a novelty emerged. They lost control over the species that would one day take over the planet's fate – what they never thought to be possible at that time. Because of this, we have been kept in ignorance in relation to this aspect of the issue, as well as concerning everything else.

Due to the direct responsibility of those beings who, despite being lords of life (Brahma, Vishnu, and Shiva). At the time of the facts, I still did not see that the gods' ex-pets (Homo Sapiens) now awaken to rationality. They would dominate the world, a particular set of genetic sequences appeared – artfully manipulated – in the human genome, which causes certain people to become monstrous when they assume power.

But others in inheriting the warmongering genetic sequence, elitists and dominators, arising from the ancestral disputes of the dominant Castes – who have been at war for power many times – philosophically impaired ideologies in their ethical essence would emerge among humans. Such as Nazism, fascism, and the mediocre side of communism, which is expressed through the dictatorship of the proletariat, which, in practice, is as monstrous and corrupt as any other dictatorship.

I refer to one of the faces that I consider mediocre in communist doctrine because I think that there is another profile of this system, still to be perceived and experienced when the human being is free of the genetic marking that awakens the superlative greed and corruption by power.

In point of view, Brahma/Yahweh, Vishnu, Shiva, and their descendants belonging to the aristocracy around Trimurti are the terrible causes of totalitarian diseases, which have devastated human sensitivity, creativity, and dignity.

The authoritarian genetic sequences, which began to disfigure human nature, came exactly from the filthy game, from these bankrupted beings, from choosing humans who were the useful innocents of the moment, or even the useful idiots, who sold their souls to be elected by those beings – common aspect to the times of the past, only partly known. Regrettably and most notably, the biblical God tormented those elected, as many of them refused to be the Chosen People, which they accepted only after the long journey of subjugation that this Being and his angels applied to humans. They ended up contributing to the manipulation of human genetics to follow its sad course in such a crazy direction, intended by the Lords of Trimurti.

These totalitarian genetics inevitably began to produce the conniving silence of many of the agents of life who, in order to live better, closed their eyes to the stage of horrors that were inoculated in the human psyche.

For many centuries when barbarism was the state policy of all human settlements, and the lack of decent laws also underlined the backwardness of those days. The silence of many or all was understandable. However, in these times when the age of knowledge makes the daily facts of life available to the eyes of many human beings. It is even despairing to realize how anesthetized we are, and we continue with a kind of disturbing silence. Which degree of omission and cowardice cannot be measured? Why? Because, now, human groups seem to have their favorite corrupt monsters and dictators, according to the crude political coloring of left or right that can be attributed to them by the sick vision of a flock whose cross-eyed gaze only sees this tragic existential dichotomy.

Martin Luther King had this same perception when he said, at the time when he was alone fighting against racism in the United States.

"What worries us the most is not the shout of the violent, nor of the corrupt, nor of the dishonest, nor of the non-character, nor of the unethical. What worries me is the silence of good men".

Good? – I wonder.

It is necessary to resist the distortions and deviations that totalitarian genetics have caused in humanity's psyche.

19th Verification

We need to understand that absurdity can only be perceived by profound philosophy since the simple religious belief and ideological fundamentalism promotes this totalitarian and unbearable life model.

Profound philosophy may architect a noble motive worth living for despite everything.

Human childishness and herd behavior are the blue pills[64] to feed life and illusions. The study of philosophy helps us in the construction of the red pill[65], which we need to take for our personal growth.

Unfortunately, chiche such as for a more just society, for the good of all, among others, can be used – and they are – for the worst types of scoundrels, transvestite as left and right, that this humanity has ever produced.

An adult reading of the facts allows the spiritual adulthood enabled those to see but only for those who are promoted to know the agenda of life.

Let's face it. It is about time we leave the stage of spiritual childhood, which we have been subjected to for a long time.

Therefore, we need to realize that the totalitarian genetics of the world's religious and ideological elites needs to be faced, not with violent revolutions, but with enlightened knowledge, the only way of building a future without making the same mistakes from the past.

When humans inherited the Caste system as a way of life, they hardly knew that what was at stake was the old problem of those who rule (always the strongest) and those who obey (always the weakest). After all, the ancient Aryans replicated, in their customs, only the reaffirmation

---

[64] Blue pill refers to a human that is not aware of the true nature of the Matrix.

[65] Redpill refers to a human that is aware in the Matrix. Morpheus talking to Neo.

that totalitarian genetics prevails (in the wealthy and powerful Castes), and the rest obeys.

Nazism arose out of this seed, constantly fertilized by the shape of particular consciences that are always corrupted to conquer power. To achieve this goal, some of them turn into monsters and are actually very good at this shameful job.

It is an old disease of the Creator, passed on to Demo beings' class, and tragically inherited by Humanity.

7. Intersideral Genetic Crossbreeding

At the same time, two distinct scenarios were taking place on Earth. The first, crossbreeding of the different Demonic genus that comes from the parallel universe to ours, saw their genetics being crossbreed with the humans (Demo + Homo = Biodemol) as if invisible hands were manipulating their lives in that sense.

The second crossbreeding had extraterrestrial roots of our own biological universe being mixed with those of the condition of the Hyperborean people (Biodemol) and Homo Sapiens.

In the further North, in the Hyperborean lands, now considered legendary, another crossbreeding was occurring that I will not explain here, but I want to give the reader the information that the Lucifer Rebellion end up here on Earth planet. My trilogy *Terra Atlantis* was published for now only in Portuguese. I go into details at *Lucifer Rebellion*. In this trilogy, I described that Biodemo beings were not the only ones because of beings from another cosmic strain, such as the Nephilim, mentioned in the Jewish Bible. And the Syrian amphibians (I think this is new information for many) found themselves crossbreeding with the Human genome due to the deployment of their colonizing postures when they land on our planet and interacted with the local elements.

Some people considered Atlantis, distributed in many islands, mainly in the southern hemisphere (here again new information) of the planet, part of which composed some of the panels of Atlantic history.

Were these the only crossbreed that occurred? No! According to the information I have, there were at least 8 groups, but they are considered mythological.

In addition to these, it is good that the reader does not forget that Demonic beings, alone, dominated many other areas of Earth and were responsible for many other pages of the Atlantis past history like Mu[66]'s legendary land in the Pacific Ocean is another part of it.

The fact is that irony or destiny. With critical sense and emotional, philosophical reason awakened, the modern rationalized human was woven into this crucible of genetic crossbreeding of beings who found themselves coexisting on Earth, driven by different reasons to get here.

This aspect of the question shows no special honor for the genesis of the Humans of the Earth even though we have been conditioned to think that someone very special

---

[66] Mu: the legend of the lost continent from which the Egyptians and Mayans came. This continent, located in the Pacific Ocean between Asia and America was once considered the cradle of civilization and the reason why such distant cultures have common ground.

created us. Like a loving and wonderful God in every way. The true God, the Loving Father, seems to have nothing to do with these books falsely considered sacred by our naive ancestors, much less with what happened or is happening on Earth. In other words, it was not a noble or decent reason that eventually led the Earth Humans to be the kind of humans they are today.

I want to quote the book *Norse Mythology* by Neil Gaiman again. In this part, he talks about the unpleasant and strange analogy to glimpse a clue of how Humans emerged in the vat of molecular mixture with genetic source codes, defining species and individuals, page 125.

Do you wonder where poetry comes from? Where do we get the songs we sing and the tales we tell? Do you ever ask yourself how some people can dream great, wise, beautiful dreams and pass those dreams on as poetry to the world, to be sung and retold as long as the sun rises and sets, as long as the moon will wax and wane? Have you ever wondered why some people make beautiful songs and poems and tales, and some of us do not?

It is a long story, and it does no credit to anyone: there is murder in it, and trickery, lies and foolishness, seduction and pursuit. Listen.

It began not long after dawn time, in a war between the gods: the Aesir fought the Vanir. The Aesir were warlike gods of battle and conquest; the Vanir were softer, brother and sister gods and goddesses who made the soil fertile and plants grow, but none the less powerful for that.

The gods of the Vanir and the Aesir were too well matched. Neither side could win a war. And more than that, as they fought, they realized that each side needed the other: that there is no joy in a brave battle unless you have fine fields and farms to feed you in the feasting that follows.

They come together to negotiate peace, and once the negotiations were concluded, they marked their truce by each of them, Aesir and Vanir alike, one by one spitting into a vat. As their spit mingled, so was their agreement made binding.

Then the gods had a feast. Food was eaten, mead was drunk, and they caroused and joked and talked and boasted and laughed as the fire become glowing coals until the sun crept up above the horizon. Then, as the Aesir and the Vanir roused themselves to leave, to wrap themselves in furs and cloth and step out into the crisp snow and the morning mist, Odin said, "It would be a shame to leave our mingled spittle behind us."

Frey and Freya, brother and sister, were leaders of the Vanir who would stay with the Aesir in Asgard from now on, under the terms of the truce. They nodded. "We could make something from it," said Freya, and she reached into the vat[67].

The spittle transformed and took shape as her fingers moved, and in moments it had taken on the appearance of a man and stood naked before them.

"You are Kvasir, "said Odin. "Do you know who I am?"

"You are Odin all-highest," said Kvasir. "You are Grimnir and Third. You have other names, too many to list in this place, but I know them all, and I know the poems and chants and the kennings that go with them."

Kvasir, made of the joining of the Aesir and the Vanir, was the wisest of the gods: he combined head and heart. The gods jostled each other to be the next to ask him questions, and his answers to them were always wise. He observed keenly, and he interpreted what he saw correctly.

---

[67] Vat a small recepticle that holds holy water.

Soon enough, Kvasir turned to the gods and said, “I am going to travel now. I am going to see the nine worlds, see Midgard. There are questions to be answered that I have not yet been asked.”

“But will you come back to us?” They asked.

“I will come back, “said Kvasir. “There is the mystery of the net, after all, which one day will need to be untangled.”

“The what?” asked Thor. But Kvasie merely smiled, and he left the gods puzzling over his words, and he put on a traveling cloak, and he left Asgard and walked the rainbow bridge.

In Neil Gaiman’s book *Norse Mythology*, we see strange, bizarre, and even fictional to the current standard of human knowledge. We take it as mythology.

Our human understanding today cannot accept what is written here as reality. But it seems that it was, and here they created a being called Kvasir from their spit.

20th Verification

The gods were surprised by Kvasir's unexpected creation, as they had no idea what they were doing. We can make an analogy with what happened to Brahma/Yahweh, one of the gods, when he saw the Homo Sapiens genus appearing on Earth.

Let’s replace the saliva of the gods with other emanations common to these beings. We will see that, in the case of humans, another type of hybridism took place.

This crossbreeding caused a great surprise when they perceived the type of rationalized, shrewd, critical, and loving being which arose from a somewhat fortuitous mixture and, paradoxically, on the other hand, also programmed with genes, although it was not known what result in it would produce.

Humans will know the evolutionary leaps that took place within the scope of this Creation in a short time. The creation of the two universes was always produced based on the randomness of the dice game. Which results were crossbreeding as a natural consequence of life's events? Alternated the processes of new possibilities promoted by the empire of the hour.

In the case of the Biodemos beings that came to Earth as an offshoot of the Lucifer Rebellion, of the few leftovers, those from the North, who had joined the Hyperborean people, gradually withered away. Because they belong to what the Hyperborean hybrid people considered to be original beings from an ancestral history, they were also seen as gods in some of that nucleus.

The Biodemos arrived on Earth well before the arising of the miscegenation of people emerging from the genetic crossbreeding that came to exist on this planet.

In other words, these Biodemos beings came to be remembered as ancestral divine beings by Hyperborean people – who, for the most part, were born on Earth – for being considered originally from the outside, peaceful, and much more enlightened than the first of these Hyperborean people, that's why they functioned as mentors at the beginning of this civilization.

I wonder if insert beings as gods is a common criterion in the universe? We have different patterns of ancestrality among the cosmic genus, so why divinize them as gods?

Without going into the merits of the issue. It appears that the first generations of Earth Humans were inclined to worship because they were led to this by an intermittent series of strategic events, promoted exactly aiming to dominate by fear.

The first terrestrial men and women were conditioned in many ways and, in particular, as a way of feeling protected, thus aligning the reason for their existence to a process that was already underway, which gave tones of naturalness to the domain of gods over Humans – who, although already rational, were ignorant and naive, since inexperienced because they were newcomers.

It should also be noted that the Biodemos never felt any inclination to worship or venerate even the very figure of Sophia[68], known as the direct creator of all families.

There are those who think, however, that the Earth Humans have already emerged for life with the inclination to worship written in their genome, and that is why the need for someone like Pandora, Pyrrha[69], and Eve[70] to mutate the area of human DNA that showed this tendency – there inscribed by the genetic manipulations of the most

---

[68] Sophia the being that was in charge when the Lucifer Rebilion happened. He is known as all knowledge and philosophy.

[69] Pyrrha was the daughter of Epimetheus and Pandora and wife of Deucalion.

[70] Eve in the Book of Genesis in the Hebrew Bible and Quran was the first woman.

evolved beings in the field of intelligence. But not in the emotional and philosophical ones, which also make up the psyche of beings. Probably, therefore the waves of Humans'creations were slow as if woven to be trained later.

21st Verification:

Things happened simultaneously, as well as the first waves of Humans appeared on the Earth with their crossbreeding as well as in parallel were produced more prototypes.

All of this evidence is in reach for classical science. But still, they make the absolute point of formulating awkward explanations to justify the evolutionary parameters and the absence of transition fossils. At the same time, in university cellars, they hide skeletons and prefer to camouflage instead of searching for the truth they present not to lose the flow of funds. Although exposed to our reach, the past has never been adequately observed through the eyes of scientific classicism.

Actually, judging the past with the eyes of the present is always an inglorious and even unproductive task as to the results of the analyzes made, because the obvious of today seeks to frame what it finds strange, and, so, the predetermination of what is to be found as a result is already established, even though the entire set of evidence negates what is now stated to be true.

The mistaken premise of this classicism that there was never the presence of extraterrestrials in the planetary past due to the simple fact that this same orthodox look does not admit that they exist; just this puts down any serious study about the past.

Regardless of what the current doctors of the law might think about it, everything indicates that, in the distant past, even before the appearance of the rational Earth Human, Demo beings. Coming from a universe parallel to ours, therefore, as already said, extra physical, the Biodemos beings, natural from our biological universe, although asexual, and some classes of the Biodemol genus, also natural from our universe, being animalized and sexed ended up settling on Earth, guided by several reasons.

Crossbreeding diverse cosmic origins occur in many worlds of the universe. But that only implies a peaceful and orderly coexistence within the values standards of somewhat robotic civilizations that populate the circuits of these worlds-stations, or worlds of diverse interactions and exchanges. Obviously, there are also problems, but not among societies manipulated in this sense.

22nd Verification

On Earth, however, several stages of a unique type of crossbreeding took place, the mixture with Demo, Biodemo, and Biodemol being that comes to Earth and with the elements of the local nature, which, in the end, over the last 8,000 years, has resulted in 2 types of people.

1. The hybrid people of the Hyperborean.
2. The Human people of whose species only one service, the Homo Sapiens, even though they don't know how to tell its story.

Perhaps the time has come for this humanity to understand their nature, regardless of who created us. Violence was the form of survival that was legitimized and forced the strongest to rule over the weakest.

This aspect of existence, which is found in the defining source code of universal life, only seems to have been abolished by the biological robotization that makes, for example, the bees in a hive look life, feel good about dedicating their lives so that the queen bee fulfills its function.

According to this perspective, the bee civilization that lives under the protection of a similar genetic pattern can continually evolve technologically. Everyone will be fine, as long as there are no dissatisfactions, even if they are programmed exactly just to feel good that way.

23rd Verification

The Hyperborean hybrid people had a very slight dose of unsealing[71], which made the Demo forces, through their avatars, find a way to reorganize those societies. This is how we can understand today how the Caste regime started taking place on Earth.

The missing link, which connects the current Earth Human with the ancestry that slowly led them to be what they are today, corresponds to the pattern of Hyperborean people. They come down from the extreme North to the more temperate regions – such as those of present-day called Ireland, Scotland, and various parts of the Scandinavian peninsula – originated what today is mistakenly called mythology.

The so-called Celtic, Nordic, Germanic, Finnish-Ugrian, Aryan mythologies, among others, are nothing more than representations of the cultural traditions. That had transmitted to the knowledge of humanity. An imperceptible missing link that has been transformed into diverse legends.

Mythical tales talk about some kind of unsealing that has taken place whenever dissatisfaction arises. And this is more or less what represented the awakening of Human rationality in relation to the entire universal conjuncture surrounding it.

[71] Unsealing, the beings created by Trimurti had their brain sealed so that they could not disobey. Here the Hyperborean had a very slight dose of unsealing.

As some Human nuclei were dominated and miscegenated, in some way, by and with beings from outside – notably the Hyperboreans – the inheritance of the Castes was also carried on through the Aryan descendants of Gomer, as mentioned before.

24th Verification

I am taking a look from the perspective of the creators of the Caste system. The majority of those beings come from outside – the antimaterial parallel universe. The aspect of good and evil was never in question.

What, then, would be their organizational and political perspective? Beings of this psychic type always move around the conceptual notion of order and chaos related to their environment. As well as, and mainly, to the degree of disturbance that can arise, impacting the way they usually live. When the structure is broken, and disorder is established. That's how they move their psychism!

They were essentially aiming at the evolution of some Demo nucleus – which, in the opening of the portals that took place in the cosmic evolution. They learned to transit between the antimaterial universe where they live and ours, the material – the Hyperborean people newly emerged on the face of the planet, and the avatar Krishna starts work the concept of order and chaos.

By the time, life had a duration that seems like fiction compared to the normal standards that today move Earth's psyche. Because of the pattern that was common for bodies associated with the Demo genetics. They live for about seventeen thousand years.

Lord Krishna coexisted, taught, dueled, killed, and suppressed what, in his judgment, was the entrenchment that the dark Demo forces had managed to establish on Earth in order to face the hosts of good. These latter organized themselves, under his coordination, for the great and decisive battle between order and chaos – and not between good and evil. Human translators interpreted – in the sense that, depending on which side was victorious, it would define whether the Earth would be inherited by the dark Demo hosts or by those who represented the order.

This perspective is simplistic, but it is the only way that, until now, has been found of talking about this subject with unsuspecting humans.

Using the concepts of light and darkness, good and evil have been the common bias on the transition between Demonic and Human. The Demodharmic culture stagnated but managed to transfer part of its canons or precepts to humans, who surprisingly inherited the Earth. The battle between order and chaos was to see which of the two Demo hosts, the enlightened one on the issue of its Dharma and the one that was confused in this regard, would inherit the planet. That was the background of the Mahabharata!

Unexpectedly, this Demodharmic cultural heritage remained for humans, which transformed Demo protagonists into heroic humans – which does not correspond to the truth.

Besides, another aspect of the problem is that, in the standards of human culture, Demo beings came to be considered bad and Angelic beings good, when before, there was a natural concept of good and bad Angels, good and bad Demons, as well as the notion of good and bad gods.

It should be noted that the concept of God the Most Loving Father never existed in that past, being a recent theological creation, perhaps because the figures of the Biblical God, the Hindu gods, never seemed to favor western sensibility.

It was in a very different context from what is now happening on Earth that some ancient cities dictated the course of events – today submerged by the advance of the seas with the melting of the accumulated ice, promoted by the increase of the temperature in the scope of the planetary surface.

One of them, located in present-day India, was one of the cities that Lord Krishna chose as the stage for his performance, when the strangest intersidereal genetic crossbreeding pattern ever occurred in the universe, according to the annals of the Demo culture.

Krishna, a Keshava Biodemol avatar in a certain order of perspectives, was present in this world exactly when the war described in the Mahabharata – Hindu epic that everyone who seeks the truth should know and study.

25th Verification

Lord Krishna was the great formulator, revelator, executor, and main definer of Dharma and Varna's issues for the Demo people and their Hyperborean descendants, who started living on Earth.

As he explained to Arjuna, in chapter IV of the *Bhagavad Gita*, it was up to him to institute the Caste system at a time well before his personality as Krishna.

Lord Krishna says.

I taught Vivasvan this eternal and transcendental science of Yoga. Vivasvan passed it on to Manu, the father of all men, and he then passed it on to Ikhsvaku, king of this world.

This supreme science was passed on through the chain of succession, and it was thus received also by devout kings. But as time went by, the chain was interrupted, and science as such was lost.

Today I am revealing to you this ancient science of union with the Supreme because you are My devotee and also My friend, and can therefore understand its transcendental mystery.

Even though I am not born, my imperishable body cannot be corrupted; although I am Lord of all living beings, I manifest My original form when needed.

Whenever dharma declines and adharma prevails, I manifest myself, oh descendant of Bharata.

To re-establish dharma, save the devotees, and annihilate the wicked, I appear in every age.

Being free from attachment, without feeling hate or fear, and always thinking of Me, many have purified themselves by knowing or penance, achieving love for Me.

I reward each one as one surrenders to Me, O descendant of Pritha. But in any case, everyone follows Me.

I instituted the four Castes according to the division of qualities and actions. Know that I am its author (my emphasis). I am, however, inactive and immutable.

Works do not contaminate me, nor is their fruit an object of desire for me; his actions do not bind the one who knows Me.

Knowing this, the former aspirants for liberation fulfilled their duties. You should also act as they did in the past.

When we understand that Krishna's words refer to a Demonic context, the consequences of which ended up on Earth, involving some Hyperborean people and others that, at that time, existed here, it will be easier to understand the pedagogical side of teaching Dharma for those beings whose nature still needed to be aligned with philosophical principles.

The apparent aspect that the events of those days previous 8,000 years ago did not have humans as protagonists – because these were simple pets' animals. But, hybrid beings, between the Demonic and the Biological-homo condition, which unfortunately ceased to exist for those who would come to know that history many millennia later, as was the case with Human culture, which, strangely, ended up inheriting the Earth.

The strange aspect here refers to the fact that, among the many thinking species that lived on Earth at the time, especially the powerful non-human, it was up to exactly the only one that had no mental power of any order to inherit the planet.

Unfortunately, modern historians have never understood this aspect, starting from the mistaken premise that only humans exist as thinking beings and have not understood the past.

Mythologies have been transformed into legends and works of art in the field of fiction; current generations of human beings have lost the ability to see the obvious of a most compelling question for those who seek the truth, although this, at first, really disturbs the seeker’s psyche.

The disturbing impact of the false peace of those who think they have found the truth in their religions is expressed when the adult understanding of the Creator's downfall is possible. His desperate process of personal reconstruction – today called Brahma by the ancient Aryans / Hindus, Yahweh by Jews and Christians, and Allah by Islamists –made him the personification of chaos, and it is not surprising that, in Greek mythology, it is called like that.

Remember the possible reader of these pages that, for the Demo mentality, the worst thing that could exist was not evil, but chaos. Brahma was organizing himself and his Creation, or in other words, organizing the chaos that is his work, where the tasks that the great beings endeavored to solve, Krishna is one of the main architects and executor of that process.

26th Verification

The problem was that a difficult task was placed on the shoulders of Humans; they inherited the problem of reconstructing the chaos.

In these hybrid beings' culture, these tasks came to be called Dharma or sacred duty. It was exactly one of these, a big job that Krishna sought to perform, teaching and even convincing Arjuna, in the Bhagavad Gita, an integral part of the Mahabharata, to fulfill his part, however unpleasant it would be to destroy his cousins, who disputed the monarchical succession power.

Dharma, therefore, was established with Hyperborean people – I'll repeat it, the great missing link between current humans and the central theme focused on in this book – as a way to allow progress that could never exist due to the failure of the portion of the Demo genetics defining source code, existing in the bodies of those hybrid beings.

This subject should be better understood in the future. Here, I only have to introduce it to provide reflection for future generations of humans who can validate or not what is exposed on these pages.

When the failure of the millennial tradition of the Demo culture occurred, and humans inherited such Caste patterns, they were unable to have any critical notion about it, which is why, today, at the tip of this Dharmic lineage, today India is completely victimized by this process.

This implies that those who are subjected to the Caste regime think exactly around the same patterns of the hybrid people from the past, which turns out to be, at least, problematic. After all, we are talking about a delay, about a great stagnation around a process that met the needs of demonic brains and minds, and not humans. We are pretty different and much more complex than our ancestors in what concerns the type of brain our species has and the evolutionary possibilities that the mental program, which arose together with Human nature, provides in the field of evolution.

27th Verification

Some characters of history like Pandora, in the view of Greek mythology. In the Christian tradition, Adam and Eve may have been the first creatures whose personal consciences awoke to the notion of good and evil. They are in different times in history. These awaken neither the Angels of the Creator nor the Demo beings could ever conceive.

Finally, we substitute concepts such as order and chaos with good and evil because we value our emotions with notions of moral nobility. Demonic beings and their descendants – even the first biological civilizations in this universe – never managed to formulate these concepts.

There is a divine favor in the fulfillment of the tasks that creatures do for these gods!

The problem is that their Demo forms have not yet become aware of it or, if they did, they still disguise it today, as if charging for the old coin of gratitude that the creatures must offer to the gods for having generated them.

Such ignorance!

And so, there is Darma and fulfillment of absurd karmic tasks, which only represent the law of the hive, where everyone works for a few or even for one.

28th Verification

Misapplied Dharma is the misguided and simplistic Demo understanding product, which is affected by existential stupidity.

That is why Dharma, for many, legitimizes Caste among humans when it was only a system to be well applied with Demo or Hybrids of their lineage.

Unfortunately, many educated men and women, but still prisoners of the old Eastern vision, defend the execrable Caste thesis as if this system's perpetuation were something worth thinking about by spiritually progressive people.

8. Transition to Human Culture

At this point in this present work. I need to establish a parameter that better identifies a mysterious transition process on Earth. At that time, there was an open connection between the lokas[72] of the Demos there in the antimatter universe parallel to ours with the surface of the planet earth here in our material universe.

For a better understanding, I will have to make a mixture somewhat complex. When the Creation starts, those beings look like animals to humans of today. Diverse breeds and crossbreeding did compose those animalize beings without awareness of themselves—ancient animals and Demonized beings, with their multiple psychological patterns.

When studying intelligence evolution, scientists start from the premise that a reasonably advanced intelligence boasts a considerable level of self-awareness, which allows it to recognize itself in the mirror. However, it does not mean that beings who are unable to have a

[72] **Loka** (Sanskrit) is a concept in Indian religions, that means plane or realm of existence.

certain self-awareness do not have intelligence levels for other purposes.

Following this perspective, few species have managed to evolve within the scope of terrestrial nature. In addition to our own Human Species, chimpanzees, orangutans, gorillas, elephants, dolphins, orcas, and magpies[73] - are examples of animals that recognize themselves as individuals. A common point among these species is that their members are social. But not in the same sense as in other species considered highly social, such as ants, termites, and bees – insects that organize themselves in the form of totalitarian colonies, with a strict division of labor and functions.

In these species of insects, a single individual – the Queen of the colony – has reproductive rights and keeps under its submission everything else – even concerning the lives of the other inhabitants of the anthill, hive, or termite mound.

What does this have to do with the central theme of this book? It would not be unreasonable to say that, by analogy, the Queen Bee is for worker bees, just what Yahweh is for his creatures.

I will emphasize that there was an intermediate genus between the Demo and Homo genus.

Which members were more like the type of being that would not recognize itself in the mirror and, despite having traces of the affected psyche of the Demons? They

[73] Magpies are birds of the Corvidae family.

were trained to obey through the harsh discipline that came from the orders of a Demon king or Demon Queen of that lineage, who completely dominated the lives of its members.

Time will come when humans will know that almost all of the oldest civilizations, which came through this universe, had this type of source code in its basic root, which has always worked in the dictatorial model.

First, there was a whole context of a Clone/Demo[74] history, which took place in the universe parallel to ours. In which the mental seal of the Cloned beings was broken there at the beginning of times when a rebel Angel-clone confronted the Creator. This conflict resulted in demodharmic beings' appearance, who started to enjoy certain mental independence, although with dementia and cancer problems in their personal (mental-corporal) organizations. I have several books on those subjects, most for right now in Portuguese.

The defining source code with the nature of the Creator, a Clone Demo version of it, was transmuted from the antimaterial universe to ours, material and biological. This code gave rise to diverse civilizations in many worlds, all of them obedient and dependent on what this source code brought as the limit of freedom that the first species displayed (and there was almost no freedom).

---

[74] Clone/Demo are the first being of Brahma's creation and in the future they will be known as the Angels.

Lucifer Rebellion was about breaking the mental seals. They run away and end up here on Earth.

In this way, the dictatorial genetic model imported into our universe found the rebels here offering resistance. With the Biodemo beings, these limits were overcome. That led to the emergence of the Human Species that is now seen on Earth.

The Varnas system was, therefore, the natural first moments' portrait of a transition. The dictatorial model that was used to Demos was transferred here. And everything was implemented to aim at hybrid beings, and this heritage fell on Human shoulders, as in our brothers and sisters of India.

So, on Earth, what later came to be known as Caste practices in some parts of India was a simple unfolding of a strong dictatorship political-social pattern. This event brought with it the emergence of the psyche with simplistic characteristics and blind obedience, an aspect that has come to exist and still exists in these species in a sadly exuberant way, including in the Earth Humans.

In other words, what has been exposed so far, at the time when the Trimurtian entities – descendants of the Hindu triad (Brahma, Shiva, and Vishnu) or the Greek triad (Chaos, Tartarus, and Eros), regarded as mythological Demons from the past – dominated the Earth, when humans had not even been organized into the nucleus by their extraterrestrial mentors or even on their own initiative. There was a set of two main biases, among others, in the segment of our genome, which guided our psyche. These genetic sequences were responsible for the unusual capacity for creativity and the amazing sense of freedom that led humans to do everything in their search for it. This differential, so common to the human characteristic, took a specific time to be noticed by the non-human beings, who were anchored in the ocean.

Only after a certain point in this story was Trimurtian beings perceived – with knowledge for it – a latent potential in Earth Humans, never seen in Demodharmic or Trimurtian culture.

How did it happen? The two titan brothers, Prometheus[75] and Epimetheus[76] , long before the appearance of human beings on the face of the Earth, found that a creativity gene existed discreetly in some segments of the Olympian-Trimurtian Society. This gene was not present in other Demo beings. Later, this was related to the fact that a strange freedom gene also existed in the very few that were minimally creative, while in other segments, this gene was absent.

Over time in antimaterial reality, which Trimurtian beings have always lived in, it was considered normal and common the perception that the existence of the genetic segment of creativity seemed to be related to the freedom one; that is, among the Demo, there were those with

[75] Prometheurs had assigned his brother Epimetheus the task of populating the earth with animals and men. Greek mythology.

[76] Epimetheus appeared as a foolish caracter, while Prometheus was the clever one. They are a pair of Titans who "acted as representatives of mankind" (Kerenyi 1951, p 207).

tendencies towards greater mental freedom (which were also somewhat creative) and those less inclined to have such impulses.

When Humans first emerged and were still irrational, Epimetheus began collecting them as his domestic animals, training them in many of the interactive ways with the life they used to have. In their experiments with their Human guinea pigs, Epimetheus and his brother Prometheus used potions or drinks that contained the sequences of the areas of the Demo genome that were programmed for mental freedom. They wanted to see how it could stimulate the most intelligent animals among those that existed under the control of Epimetheus to become creative to find solutions to primary challenges and everyday needs.

So, to fix the information, for a long time of that reality, in antimaterial history or Demo history of Creation (or even Demodharmic culture), there is a context in which the Demonic way of being prevailed over that of Cloned beings – the Clone Angels, due to the evolutionary inertia of being simple electromagnetic robots, shaped by the mind of the fallen Creator.

The Demo prevailed and shaped their culture through the billions of years; in the beginning, they were Clone.

Demonic life was being woven into the antimaterial universe, parallel to ours. In contrast, life didn't even exist in the one. We live, since it only appeared, in its chemical-biological version, after the third generation of stars sowed the heaviest chemical elements and carbon in particular – which are forged notably in the final period of the stars' lives, during the final explosions of their cycle.

There is, therefore, a Demo version about this Creation, but when intelligent chemical beings and, mainly, rationalized biological ones appeared in the material universe, a slow elaboration of a rationalized version about the same universal Creation and of the facts that occurred on Earth began. It should be noted that biblical Anunnaki or Nephilim have their own version of the facts.

Among all these, there is also the Earth Human version, totally wrong, which is the most recently elaborated – because Humans of Earth are the youngest race to emerge within this universe, and it seems to be the most special one – and it was built in our historical past, but poisoned by the interference of the Demo, who intended the domination of the humans.

Complicating the perspective of analysis from the current generations of Earth Humans, when all other thinking species operating on Earth were prevented from continuing to pursue their goals of domination or shared colonization, observing that their former smart animals of petting and slavery have multiplied beyond their control systems then used, have decided to interfere in human culture, which has recently emerged through the awakening of rationalization – promoted by Pandora – poisoning it in such a way that it has led the new generations of human-thinkers in post-Socratic Greece to consider the news about gods as legendary tales and, more recently, these have been classified as mythologies.

The Illuminism and modern and postmodern versions of what is rational and what is not, even though quantum postulates have been disturbing this anachronistic and outdated materialistic belief for more than a century, buried an old context that was turned into unreal, even if its effects last until today – and they will continue in the future – like it or not authors who have come to be considered classic.

Unfortunately, it is up to me to affirm that their points of view, their premises, and the logic of their arguments are absolutely wrong because they consider a past context that is extremely real and complex beyond measure to be unreal.

Modern thinkers managed to believe and worked hard for it that a very rich and complex compendium, yet considered by them as fake, about the first news concerning both universal and Human ancestry is only the product of the exaggerated Human mind – which was and is the major factor responsible for the way Earth Humans's psyche works. They even sneakily assert that the issue is not about it being true or false, but about it being a mere literary creation, which occurred in antiquity, at the root of Human culture evolution.

Honestly, I don't know where the most significant degree of ignorance or even dogmatism (caged knowledge) is found when the so-called scientific thought about this issue imposes on the orthodoxy of the times, whether in the use of the history subject, which is intended to be scientific, but which works apart from the archaeological remains themselves, or whether in the pride of the self-proclaimed doctors about their favorite legends and versions that, by the authority they think they are invested with, they confuse their personal views with the history they sell in their books.

Worse, those who think according to academic standards are considered normal, and this is a correct attitude even if it is linked to historical lies. The contrary thinking is considered abnormal, heretical, and without credibility because it is removed from the scientific canon, although it is factually correct.

One of the aspects of the universal drama and of all the species that live within this problematic Creation is that the truth takes time to free itself from the control exercised by the canons of each epoch and each place with the power of the cosmic moment, which always slows down the evolutionary process and punishes the most evolved beings, in addition to bringing together those subjected to the belief with the convenience of the establishment control.

Faced with this context, the human version of Creation and the meaning of life is totally under the control of religions, for believers, and academically enthroned scientism, for its adherents. In contrast, those who are situated beyond these controls are beaten from all sides, in their sensitivity, in addition to being branded with no credibility to address such issues – meaning those who take from the religious and scientific segments the elements not affected by the interests of belief and research funds, building models of transient understanding to search for truth and, most of the times, much more honest and close to a possible factual truth than that of the two historically dominant movements.

29th Verification

The guardians of the faith and the guardians of scientism are the worst that can exist. They are an obstacle to advancing human thought in the search for the truth or something that might resemble this concept.

Oh, the guardians! This habit came into existence in the human culture exactly as a direct legacy of this ancient mental habit rooted in the Demo psychic – and that, until today, causes in the Demo beings the very same obstacles that, in their dementia, prevent them from perceiving the complexity of what the critical sense and the emotions valued by the human way can lend them nowadays.

Because of these religious and scientific controls, today's Earth Humans think there are missing links of all kinds – historical, anthropological, archaeological, paleoanthropological – situated among the many evolutionary phases of our historical genesis.

30th Verification

Between the ancient Democulture (the first to appear in the realm of Creation) and the current Human culture (the last to appear in this context), there is an impressive number of intermediate cultures, including the missing links its multiple faces.

In the transition between this ancient context and the current world, much that is unknown and, therefore, strange – for our present way of thinking – happened and defined what the Earth Humans came to be.

Thus, emerged among countless families of the Demo culture, and also among the biological species of our universe, the species of the Earth humans – it's not a pleonasm because there are Humans out there, even though we don't know them – has been invaded, since its birth, by all these cultural patterns, an aspect that deeply infected what we now think is obvious of things.

31st Verification

Humans and Demos found themselves on the same road, in the middle of an evolutionary journey that passed through the Earth's stage; the system of Demo Castes, which had been working for a long time for them, began to involve humanity and became embedded in it, mainly through the local culture of Hinduism.

When humanity multiplied and began to be manipulated by the Demo gods, the Caste system remained in use, as it still is today.

Even though the Demo gods left the scene, the disgrace was already established and, as already seen in previous chapters, all due to the misinterpretation of the Aryan / Hindu traditions made of the Dharma.

Now, I will have to address the part of this transition context again, which took place between the Demo and the Homo, emphasizing new nuances of the issue.

The beings described in several books and ancient traditions of the nucleus and focus of today's human culture were exactly of the Demo Homo genus. However, in addition to the genetic Demo and Homo. The components and their hybridism, another called Biodemo– as already mentioned – was also present in this genetic breeding.

From this crossbreed, the already mentioned Hyperborean hybrid people appeared in the extreme North of the planet and lived there between 14,000 and 23,000 years ago.

The cultures called, under the Celtic perspective, like those of the cities of Fidias, Gorias, Murias, Falias, and Elixoia, among others, which gave rise to the Tuath(a) Dé Danann, which coexisted with the Partolans, with the Nemedians, besides the sons of Erin (who inhabited Northern Ireland), represent some of the ramifications of those people, among which the Caste system was in force.

After the cataclysms that occurred between 9,000 and 14,000 years ago, when humans descended from Noah's lineage, and survivors of the flood came on the scene, beyond the genetic boundaries of this offspring, other people of the Homo Sapien Sapien[77] – who inherited the genetic-cultural patterns of the hybrid people of the Hyperborean times – continued to adopt the Caste system, which even interfered in Noah's own genetics through one of his grandchildren, Gomer, ancestor of the Aryans, that saw his people receiving the influence of people located more to the East, who inhabited part of the present region of Pakistan and India.

Few realize, but the Aryan Castes are part of the oldest ancestral traditions, which ended up building, later on, the Judeo-Christian component.

The Varna/Caste aspect that already existed among the Demo groups who lived in their parallel dwellings – the lokas – was already implemented in these hybrid people, non-human. In this context, as mentioned earlier to Arjuna, Krishna's speech was registered in the Bhagavad Gita, emphasizing the advantages of that social system, as it has been partly reproduced previously.

Since then, the Castas system has been inherited by the human condition, being particularly and later concentrated among the Dravidian people of the regions of Mohenjo Daro and Harappa, due to the influence of the

---

[77] Homo Sapien Sapien is a subspecie, skull is smaller and more compact and the face is much less elongated than the Neanderthal; the modern human skull has a higher forehead, less prominent brow-ridges and smaller teeth. Modern humans are typically much less robust in body form and skeleton than Neanderthals.

migration of some Aryan tribes to the south, which would later determine its definitive transfer to Hindu culture.

The Caste systems transition road is unpleasantly tortuous as it was helpful in dominate demented Demons, yet adopting the same strategy for humans does not make any sense because of our species' nature.

Unfortunately, even avatars like Sai Baba – a Human being whose importance I cannot measure, so big he seems to be – openly defended this adaptation of the Caste system to humanity. However, I point out, in my littleness, that such a posture is a mere product of the Trimurtian Demo pollution that inevitably seems to affect, somehow, the mind of all the avatars coming from the Trimurti moves, with intentions of domination of this or that people, among the Earth Humans.

I am not going to elaborate on my comments here about Sai Baba's arguments on the issue. First, I will try to clarify what he understood as the instruments and the mental possibilities that the Human condition has to perceive the truth.

For that, I need to reproduce some of the passages recorded in books of his unforgettable lectures for people who went to his ashrams in India.

Said Sai Baba to the youth:

"Personifications of Universal Atma. Every object of creation in this world has some distinctive characteristic and its own character. If any of these objects abandon their distinctive aspect, they will self-destruct. Here are some examples of this. The fire has the ability and quality to burn. Water has the ability to flow. Man has the quality of human nature, and an animal has the quality of being raw.

When the ability to burn is gone, we cannot call it fire. When the ability to flow disappears, we cannot call it water. When the inner vision or basic human nature disappears, we cannot call him a man. When the external view or raw nature disappears, we cannot call it an animal.

So, we see that there is an inherent quality for everything, which constitutes life for that specific object. The natural quality of being human is to have an inner vision. By definition, an animal can only look externally. We can be human beings in form, but if we only have an external vision and cannot look within ourselves, we cannot be called human beings. We will be called animals.

This quality is also called the dharma of this object. This dharma takes many different forms. When any object exceeds the natural dharma or the characteristic of itself and promotes something in excess, we can call it an attempt to encourage Dharma. Just as a student, through the effort to be promoted from a specific degree to a higher degree, an individual can promote himself to a higher level by promoting his own dharma and paying attention to the highest and noblest things. "

Here the problems begin, in the field of understanding, when Sai Baba transforms what makes us human into Dharma, what we should not agree with, for accepting this as truth will be the same as inverting the concept of ethics that the philosophical postulates of Human freedom allow us to conceive.

As we will see later, it is precisely in this acceptance that he presents one of the justifications for the Caste system to exert its terrible and unjustifiable burden on Humans.

To accept his thesis is to agree with the caged human being in a function associated with duty, just as non-human beings from the immemorial past did it because of their limited varna (inclination or natural talent).

Let us continue, however, with the reproduction of the lecture of the most recent avatar - Sai Baba - who, until recently, was among humans:

"An inert piece of iron can be converted into a portion of helpful gear through successive applications of heat. From a piece

of iron that has not received proper treatment and, therefore, is worth a few changes, we can manufacture a precious watch after undergoing the necessary changes.

We must note here that it is the samskara[78] or the change we give to the substance that values it and not the raw material's inherent value.

Likewise, a simple and unsophisticated human being can obtain the opportunity to elevate himself to the position of a Paramahamsa (spiritually accomplished sage) if he seeks the company of higher beings.

The mind of man longs to obtain such sacred wisdom through the use of the sense organs. In this case, intelligence stands out, placing itself before the mind to distinguish what is good and what is bad since the mind itself cannot operate such a distinction. Even intelligence alone cannot decide between good and evil, but it

---

[78] Samskara are mental impressions, recollections or psychological imprints on Hindu philosophies. It become the basis for the development of karma theory.

is capable of judging everything that is put in front of it. In the case of a judge, we know that he will decide between good and evil based only on the facts presented to him.

Similarly, the nature of intelligence is such that it can decide between good and evil only on the basis of the facts presented to it and cannot go beyond the facts. The mind's quality is to conduct and practice dharma, and the quality of intelligence is to decide between good and evil based on the facts presented to it. But in today's world, this type of intelligence can be classified into four different categories.

These categories are: the first, the selfish type; the second, the selfish-altruistic type; the third, a purely altruistic type; and the fourth is based on the Atma. The first category is always thinking about what is good for itself and decides to be good for its own ego. The second category, which is partly selfish and partly altruistic, will think of the good for itself along with the good of others. (...) The third category, which can be described as altruistic intelligence, always thinks of others and will take into account the type of happiness desired for itself as well as the type of happiness that others should have. The kind of sadness that it wants to get rid of is also the sadness that it wants others to get rid of. (...) The fourth category – the atmabudhi (spiritualized intelligence) – is always concerned with the aspect of dharma and the need to safeguard dharma. This category always thinks of itself as a messenger from God, and in forgetting its own selfish interests, it always thinks about sacrifice and does good things for the rest of the world. In this category, only the truth has the right to decide what is good and what is bad."

Again, I emphasize the apparent and insurmountable obstacle that Sai Baba's thought imposes around the theme by placing truth as the factor that can decide what is good and what is bad.

What, then, would that truth be? Humans, which will always rest in the Dharma, in the way that he and the Hindus are conditioned to accept? It will be exactly that truth, that of Dharma as the duty of Humans to accept the prescription elaborated by Shiva / Krishna, previously, which in many other circumstances will be used to justify the Caste system among Humans.

The detail is that Shiva and the avatar Keshava Krishna dealt with the Castes among people who were not even Human. Still, the human condition of Sai Baba, an avatar of Krishna, in the first order, and Shiva in genetic precedence, does not seem to have noticed this aspect and errs in giving continuity to what does not contribute to the existential dignity of a human being. Sai Baba goes on.

> "Others have no right of making such a decision. It was in this context that our sruthis (Vedic scriptures) declared: there is no other Dharma but the truth."

Summer Roses in the Blue Mountains - Speeches by Sai Baba.

In another work, he states.

"You will only understand the importance of the endeavor to protect dharma when you consider its origin and purpose. On his own initiative, God created this Jagat and established several codes to ensure its maintenance and smooth flow, with rules of conduct for each being. These constitute Dharma."

Smooth flowing? – I have to question that!

Sai Baba also explains that Dharma is that which serves as a garment for the territory (desa) or the body (deha), that is, the function in life and the function of life in facing this jagat, referred by him.

However, what is the meaning of the Sanskrit expression Jagat? Jagat means the phenomenological world, supported by physical, chemical, and biological codes, that is, created not by god – contrary to what Sai Baba claims – but for a Being that the Hindus themselves acknowledge having been a Creator, Prajapati who, in generating a strip of reality, fell into it, becoming the reconstructed being called Brahma.

The concept of god should be absolutely different from that of Creator, an aspect that the purposeful blindness of religions, until today, prefers to hide because they cannot explain how a perfect, loving, and just god generates a nature in which all species are already born with cancer and with the murderous instinct to destroy other species, in order to sustain their lives.

Sai Baba also kept this confused indistinction at work. Whether he did it on purpose or if it was the product of demodharmic pollution, which affects the psyche of avatars, only his spiritual conscience can one day explain.

Sai Baba continues in his transliterated speeches for books produced by his followers.

"From the constituent elements of the Universe, water has movement and cold as its dharma; combustion and light are the dharma of fire. Each of the five elements has its own dharma.

Humankind protects man against decline; animality keeps animals. How can fire be fire after it is devoid of combustion and light? It must manifest its dharma in order to remain itself. When the fire loses its dharma, it is reduced to a portion of lifeless coal."

The Dharma force is responsible for removing the world from the realm of Dharma and entering the age of Dharma.

According to Sai Baba, in the *Bhagavad Gita*, Krishna is only reviving something that was disabled, that is, the Dharmoddarharana.

Krishna says to Arjuna.

"My task is to make clear to everyone the value of dharma-karma, which must be adopted after due discernment. (...) Understand dharma as Chaturvarnyam that is, as the (social) organization of the four (chatur) Castes (varnas), which are based on the predominant guna of beings. The varna system is essential for the functioning of the world (universe). (...) I established this organization to promote loka-kshema, the well-being of the world (universe)."

The conclusion, which I wish to consider transient – because future generations should better address the issue since this avatar is already in the process of returning and should be born again in India, and it will be up to his conscience to redefine or not his posture – is that these beings that still have characteristics of a Trimurtian mission, when in the Human condition, however great their mental powers may be, they can only see what they think is the hidden truth via the mistaken concept of Dharma applied to Castes, as they use it.

It was from that kind of need of an era, which became a heavy misunderstanding for Humans who unknowingly inherited Earth, that skewed and distorted psychic lens emerged from a type of Demo spirituality that, until today, works due to the Dharma, Varna, the resulting mental karma, and the extreme veneration of a religiosity that does not evolve.

I call this aspect Demodharmic culture a literary product that, until this day, imprisons Humans in Vedic, Jewish, Christian, and Islamic cages.

As for Humans who manage to break a little free from this context distorted by the belief in an Aryan, biblical, Islamic god, absolutely detached from any notion of dignity and existential ethics, they are able to glimpse a pattern of humanized spirituality, via philosophy, through adult spiritualization, and from this, something that may resemble an enlightened religion or a philosophical ideal of freedom may emerge, with a code observed by all.

I call this fruit that comes from the life of Earth Humans enlightened Human culture, which seems to be a unique product in this Creation.

32nd Verification

The Demodharma from an absurd duty to crazy needs to be replaced one day by the Homo Dharma in which there is a spiritual evolution based on human-style wisdom, free from the Demo's oddities.

Finally, and it's very unfortunate for me to emphasize it, what has been described above represents the dramatic aspect of the thinking of a human being fueled with the baggage of mental powers that the spirit of an avatar tends to display.

And the tragic thing is that an avatar always gathers people around him as if he were an incarnated god because that is exactly what most of them think they are. However, they are not! The true god has nothing to do with the oddities of Trimurti's representatives.

33rd Verification

The avatar can hardly understand that this Dharma that they say and think is the truth is just misunderstanding arising from the affectation to the Demo culture, and this so long worshiped concept by them. Thus, when they incarnate in the human condition, they drastically attack the sincere and free search for the truth because they have the Demo certainty that they already have it.

Not even Jesus escaped this when he expressed himself as the way, the truth, and the life because he was sure that he was really the envoy of the Being whom he considered to be God.

Most likely, when he made such statements, he had not yet realized that this God had problems! Even if such disturbances were extensively described in the Hebrew people's scriptures, an aspect that he only found at the limit of his pain, at the cross. When he was resurrected, he clarified this issue by sowing what was later considered Gnostic knowledge, which recognizes Creation problems and the Creator.

Unfortunately, Gnosticism fell into hatred of the Creator, that is, almost a kind of *Lucifer Rebellion Part 2*. (go to www.Pandoraunlock.com – Time in a Blink of an Eye for Lucifer Rebellion part 1.)

It is evident that, for any being, the wonderful common concept of Dharma as the rightness of conduct in the face of a moral duty that is assumed to be sacred is a factor of education and encouragement to higher conduct.

The problem lies in the misapplication of this concept for those who find themselves caged and forced to remain prisoners of a degrading situation and a social-political context. Simply for being born in a specific social segment and obliged to remain in strict compliance with that Caste's Dharma.

This practice should not be used for Human beings, whose range of talents can continually be expanded by their evolutionary effort, which is not the case with Demos – that they are unable to do due to the dementia factor that, sadly, resides in the genome of that existential genus.

Applying the Caste system to Humans in the name of Dharma is just a spiritual crime that is practiced out of absolute ignorance of what Human Nature can produce.

The avatars make such a mistake; they had already come psychically in the condition in a mental posture of never realizing the Human condition. They are caged of never realizing the difference between Demo and Homo beings – thus maintaining control over Human group – Humans took avatars as gods - for this is how Krishna and Sai Baba, among others, are considered by Humans.

It seems that trying to control the Human group has always been the problem of such gods. They had a huge surprise when they realized the type of being that appeared on Earth.

The Biblical Yahweh posture towards Adam and Eve is an emblematic example of the issue.

Whatever it may have been, the fact is that there are Human Beings in miserable conditions that are disinherited from the fate of the gods of their beliefs. Finally, there are dalits[79] in all quarters of Earth, each local culture being the product of the unfolding of particular stories within a larger planetary context.

After all, there seems to be a mysticism about misery stating that as it was in the past, it shall be in the present, as seen in the situation shown below.

---

[79] Dalits in Hinduism were seen as a fifth varna, known by the name of Panchama. They are the lowest social group in caste system.

Before basic sanitation existed, Lisbon, Portugal, was dirty and smelly. In order to clean up the problem, then, around the end of the 6th century, the "Calhandreiras"– a type of cylindrical vessel - post was established, occupied by African slaves. They were forced to go to everyone's homes to collect human waste in the "Calhandreiras"– that they carried and pouring that filth into the Tejo River. According to the chronicles of the time, at the beginning of the 17th century, the Portuguese capital had a thousand "Calhandreiras" at its service. Each received 30 réis daily, which established the profession as the lowest paid of all.

About 4 centuries later, things are not very different for countries like India, Brazil, Bangladesh, Pakistan, Afghanistan, and many others – this is no longer the case in Portugal, which standards have evolved considerably for its citizens – where its inhabitants have never managed to evolve the levels of their educational development indexes and in other fields of life. The "Calhandreiras" continue to operate, people who, regardless of sex or age, live collecting trash on the streets of Brazilian cities, or survive by collecting the filth of those who have the privilege of having a home in India, even if not sanitized, because the majority of the poor population has no home, and lives on the streets, abandoned – estimating that this god may give them something.

Such attitudes keep these and other countries in a medieval and even ancestral context, which, let's face it, is a superlative shame or, at least, should be considered like that.

However, the strange conformism that the religious elites managed to impose on the groups of this world – so much criminal imposition in that resignation – resulted in us getting used to this state of affairs, which scandalized profound people like Nietzsche[80].

Get used to the present indignity, aiming to attain the blessings of heaven later in life, or even in another incarnation, as Hindus hope to get – Hinduism claims that your best life will come if you are well conformed in the present life – seems to have been the global choice of consciousness for many men and women living on Earth.

Inevitable? Could the story have been different? Today, could humans have another posture, a very different mental attitude from that of thinking that changing things, as they are, is making everything worse, and that is why everything should remain as it has always been?

Will it be possible, despite the weight of the conditioning imposed on this humanity, an advance in the understanding and attitude of the planetary citizen, with a view to the defense of a minimum standard of dignified life even for the eternal "Calhandeiras," the eternal children of general Human incompetence in building a decent way of walking between the cradle and the grave?

---

[80] Nietzsche was a German philosopher, cutural critic, composer, poet, writer ane philologist who become one of the most influential of all modern thinkers.

Humanity has not yet realized the fact that when the extra physical Demo hosts and the extraterrestrial biological teams that intended to dominate and inherit Earth gradually realized that this ancient certainty would not be accomplished, but that those who were once their pets, strangely, would be the ones to inherit the planetary destiny, they tried to pass on as much influence as possible to the nascent human culture, aiming to influence it in their beliefs. These innocents were the earthlings in terms of life experience.

They then forged what was possible to impose on the most unfortunate of these groups and tricked the unsuspecting Humans into thinking that they were gods and that they would leave Earth for a specific time, but they would return in the future.

What would they return to? – I asked. Of the two, one, to make fraternal contact or regain the command lost on Earth.

Planetary society needs to think about this aspect of Earth's history! Many centers of what I call the invisible power within national governments have countless information and data on the UFO issue. Still, they do not have the most remote understanding of this aspect of the question that involves Earth's isolation and its imminent reintegration into cosmic coexistence, both extraterrestrial and extra physical.

In the past, some extra physical and extraterrestrial hordes have acted, transforming terrestrial humans into a herd that would end up being fatherless and motherless because their gods would depart, leaving them with the seed of a domination nostalgia, to be felt by the then abandoned Humans.

It was so well done that even 21st century UFO researchers and much more informed Humans appreciate this return. However, there must be a good deal of caution here!

Few of the extraterrestrial groups that made up, directly or indirectly, the process of colonization of the planetary past didn't play these dirty tricks on Humans since they never intended anything in the field of domination, as was the case with the Biodemo beings of the North, former rebels - who had become involved in the Lucifer Rebellion– and Syrian beings from the East, who are amphibians.

However, the other forces present on the planet did everything to condition Humans, with the Anunnaki and the portal beings performing the most unfortunate examples of this, even though, under the perspective of the cosmic events of those days, it is understandable what, then, took place.

The cultures, both of the Anunnaki and of the beings of the portals, were imposed without any major criteria on Humans and, among these, the first who sought to organize the inheritance of so much news, did so considering such beings as gods and humans as properties of the feuds and clans.

When the Castes in India came into this context, the existing fidelity in the concept of Dharma was gradually being used as praiseworthy and necessary moral posture for humans to dedicate themselves to the causes of the gods.

It may seem simple, but human conveniences were not of the most remote importance in the early days, as long as the gods were satisfied.

34th Verification:

Over time, the beings considered as gods disappeared and, then, there were the kings and emperors who demanded the same degree of fidelity from the unsuspecting humans in order to meet their ambitions, and the Human group began to be astutely led to meet these demands, without even their minimum conveniences being met by the powerful ones.

This kind of subservience on the part of the people concerning their representatives, which can always be observed in the pages of history, made the terrain of the game of life a fertile stage for totalitarian doctrines. In the 20th century, for example, people watched, experienced, and suffered the effects of these doctrines, such as Nazism, fascism, communism, in short, ideologically designed diseases with certain colors of progress, but which, in practice, have always been monstrous and criminal.

35th Verification:

Maintaining the Caste system in India is a spiritual seal of majestic stupidity that makes spiritual darkness obtain its future best soldiers – for totalitarian experiences on Earth – composed of those who disembark entirely disgusted with the Castes.

I have no way of proving or even demonstrating it. Still, the already mentioned 20th century totalitarian systems recruited the mass of their armies from these spirits that, in an astonishing quantity, disincarnated from their miserable lives in India and many other places, being sent back to the Human nucleus that, at the time of these unfortunate events, the then-existing headquarters of darkness controlled.

Fortunately, today this kind of headquarters no longer exists, but at the time, it was so that the flows of those spirits, easy to be restrained by the doing of duty, even from nations that invaded other defenseless ones, were segmented and directed to Germany, Italy, China, Russia, and Japan, in the first decades of the 20th century.

Totalitarian regimes, so common in Human Culture, were heirs to the methods of submission and Dharma control of the patterns that served for demonic beings' education.

It was from this conformism, from this handing over of humanity's destiny to gods, from this habit of believing in a heavenly life better than the one on Earth, from the ideas of fear of hell and celestial joy, from the fear of God and from the love of this same God, in short, it was from all these oddities that this simple-minded human emerged, chained like a horse, herded, at the same time corrupt and naive, obedient and rarely rebellious, infected by the mental virus of spiritual stagnation.

This simple-minded human that began to exist, I started calling Homo hierarchicus.

9. The Homo Hierarchicus

I have lived all my life in the Northeast of Brazil, and I have been able to live with the simple yet profound faith of people I love very much, whom I consider wonderful and are affections of my soul, once again found in the figures of grandparents and of a beloved mother, totally dedicated to the Catholic cult – and they did so with the most beautiful expression of their psyche. From them, I inherited the good part that I carry with me, and I always keep the deepest respect in relation to the way they practiced their belief in Jesus, the saints of the church, and, in particular, the virgin Mary.

In addition to family life, I had the privilege of also observing the simple faith of the man and woman of the countryside, whose devotion to some saints has always caused me an emotional astonishment. The sertanejos (people from the countryside), who had nothing, or very little, complained about nothing, worked hard, were extremely friendly and zealous towards visitors, offering them what little they had. In short, they were Human beings who managed to take care of several children, and they lived in the preaching and practicing of a dignified life, totally devoted to goodness, to God, to Jesus, and to Father Cícero[81], whom they considered to be a saint.

Anyway, in my life as a Northeasterner, I was able to perceive, here and there, people's faith, a faith that fortified them, that made their lives more beautiful and bearable, beliefs that redeemed them before themselves, and much of that I saw during my travels as a geology student, as a UFO researcher, as a bank employee, as a director of companies and institutions and, finally, as a speaker.

I've always felt much smaller than these people, and I still feel that way! I learned many things from them, but I could never copy the faith and belief attitude that filled their faces with adoration and devotion. In fact, I was never able to have any kind of relationship like that with God, Jesus, or any saint, non-physical being, whatever.

When I was in India, my anxiety increased greatly because what I was used to seeing in my countrymen's belief and faith seemed extremely sophisticated compared to the way Hindus worshiped their gods.

I walked as much as I could in the midst of those people, in the most diverse situations and hours of the day and night, and I never noticed any danger, any risk of aggression on the part of the impressive number of miserable, who lived on the streets because they had nowhere to go.

---

[81] Father Cicero was a Brazilian Roman Catholic priest who became a spiritual leader to the people of Northeastern Brazil.

Since I arrived there, via Mumbai (old city of Bombay), around 1:30 am, when I had to leave the international airport to go to another place where I should take a plane to Bangalore, I was forced to cross a yard around the terminal so that I could take a bus that was parked further down.

I'll never forget the impression I had while walking with my suitcases along with the crowd that was there. As I walked, that crowd was opening a ditch while looking at me with a kind of sparkle in their eyes, which I had never seen.

After my return from India, I started researching material to continue the 3 books, *The Key of the Avatar, Dew of Time,* and *The Masters of the Soul,* that I had started to produce there – which, by the way, I have not yet completed them – and that, supposedly, they should compose a trilogy that, at the time, I called *The Mysteries of India.*

I went deeper, and I could see a priestly lineage of very special spirits, who always reincarnated in India with the function of making each of its members a light to be turned on to facilitate the hard walking of those who were born there. Besides, I also realized another objective: to keep the light of Yogi enlightenment on, which was sown at the beginning of time – back in the immemorial time that Krishna referred to while talking to Arjuna.

Going further, I went even deeper, and I could see, behind that priestly lineage, the figure of Shiva, whose last incarnation as Sai Baba – but from Krishna's personal defining source code – seemed to adorn that stream of light brilliantly.

It was then that I came face to face with the Demonic reality behind absolutely all the culture coming from Aryan/Hindu mythology, as well as from the same lineage of the priest of the Lords of Trimurti.

At that point, I noticed the already mentioned Demonic or Trimurtian Castes – it´s how I started classifying them – and human being produced by them. The Homo-hierarchicus, as I named it. This being that emerged would be easily controlled by the reins of a belief that was greater than its ability to use critical sense, common to the Homo Sapiens species – but it seemed to remain in disuse for those who lived in India, at least in that sense.

I see Homo hierarchic currently subjected to militarism, to subservience demanded by the interests of manipulation of imposing religions and outdated ideologies, my sensitivity hurts when I perceive the acceptance of these contexts in the figures of a Sai Baba and others who think they know that that situation is the best that gods could and can provide for those unfortunate people who were unlucky or had the karma to be born in those circumstances.

How good it must be to have that kind of certainty that justifies indefensible crimes in the name of misconceptions about gods! However, I am unable to have them because this is only due to the unreasonable use of misguided faith and belief. As not being well-directed, I can post them in my sensibility. I am free from this type of mistake, even if I am the wrong one for those who look at me from the flock.

The pollution of Demodharmic culture, unfortunately, until today, has invaded and influences the human culture that thinks it is normal to attribute to its gods of preference all sorts of oddities and crimes and, worst of all, disastrously turning barbarism into a sacred thing.

I don't like it at all when I see Sai Baba defending the following proposition to humans in one of the books that condense his teachings.

> "First, the diamond is a dark piece of stone, a hard pebble. Only after being cut by a skilled craftsman, it becomes a multifaceted fire flame. Allow yourself to be treated the same way, as all your shadows will disappear, and you will emerge just like a shining diamond.
>
> Act with your full potential and with the fullness of your mind. Make full use of the skill, ability, courage, and confidence you have. God will not bless you.
>
> Suffering accredits you more to the Grace of the Lord. When suffering comes in waves, one over the other, rejoice because the beach is coming. Face them bravely. Do not behave like cowards who complain about some external power or are angry with the Lord."

I know that Sai Baba spoke to a countless crowd of Hindus and other needy Humans, but I still cannot applaud such gestures.

The crushing of men and women's sensitivity by religious bias is something that I firmly resist accepting and getting used to seeing this as normal.

"Ah, but that is consolation, comfort!" someone might say.

Whatever! I think I know that someone like Sai Baba expresses himself that way with the best intentions, but even so, I take it as unjustified.

Why? Very simple: as long as the human being is no longer considered the source of all the alleged purposes that govern our life, but rather, the supposed maddening gods who promoted intrigues that, until today, are the source of endless wars – between, for example, Arabs and Jews, two groups involved with promises, pacts, and election as people chosen by the biblical God – I am one of those who think that we will never build a decent way of living on Earth.

Why have we been living in political chaos for a long time, even though our little life may be doing very well? Exactly because some (terrestrial humans reclassified, by me, as Homo hierarchic) blindly obey the values that were passed on to them by this God, via their Angels, to the chosen ones of the time – Moses, among the Jews, and Muhammad, among the Arabs.

This God, as I said, chose the Aryans, when he introduced himself to them as Brahma, then he elected the Jews, showing himself as Yahweh and, more recently, he chose the Muslim Arabs, identifying himself as Allah, but clarifying it was the same God of the Jews and Aryans. Now, how long and where will this go?

If we Humans do not choose our own values and purposes, so that we consider them supreme, giving up this philosophical obligation and handing over to this God the chance of doing it for us, where will we go, and what results will we achieve, different from the outcomes we got used to seeing as normal in life? Now, let's face it!

The oppression of the Human being and the crushing of man by a society frightened by the faith in a furious God, who punishes, is incomplete antagonism with the idea that the purpose of civilizations would be to give everyone the chance of living decently as a person.

36th Verification

The great mental battle, waged from ancient times to the present day, is the struggle for the proclamation and recognition of the dignity of the rational Human being, able to critically understand the reality in which he is inserted, to love, to create, to work, to evolve, to distinguish between good and evil by his way of thinking and valuing emotions – and not to obey apparently maddened and sick beings.

For me, what matters is recognizing the dignity of the Human being, the respect for his values, and not blind submission to absurd orders and plots, whomever the author is.

Ivan Karamazov[82], Dostoievski's character, said.

"If God does not exist, everything is allowed."

Is it? – I ask you. Honestly, I don't think so! This is the kind of understanding that interests religious elites of all times, who want humans to think that everything is over if there is no belief in God. Fallacy!

Who needs the conceptual notion of a strange God who promotes the segregation of human ethnicities instead of bringing them together?

If the universalist vision is not just a quilt made from scraps of all religions and spiritualist doctrines, but a broad understanding of the customs and religious feelings of all human beings converging towards a single spiritual goal, how can we one day consider the concept of gods as a supreme value, dear to all human beings, if we continue to live in Castes, in obedience to the oddities of the immemorial past?

One aspect of our life is that the Human being has been conditioned to submit to the hierarchy of the absurd, which promotes all kinds of terror to believers, needy and unaware of the spiritual life based on philosophical codes involving noble principles and purposes of life.

Medieval scholasticism polluted the most daring notions of Greek philosophy, which is why we have

[82] Ivan Fyodorovich Karamazov is the brainiac of the 3 Karamazov brothers.

become orphans of a broader understanding of the existence we carry. This is because it replaced the notion that belief in gods and not philosophical reflection could save the human condition from eternal damnation.

Regarding the issue of the Christian promise of salvation, in disagreement with salvation from a philosophical point of view, Luc Ferry[83] offers us a very interesting reflection:

"Christianity's victory over philosophy is evident throughout the Middle Ages: philosophy will be reduced to what we call "scholasticism," that is, it will practically no longer have the right to be interested in the question of the good life and salvation, which had become an absolute monopoly of religion. Philosophy will be reduced to an ordinary analysis of concepts, but it will no longer be, as in the great Greek schools' days, a concrete exercise in learning life.

It will be necessary to wait for the 17th century for philosophy to gradually resume, mainly thanks to Espinoza, the Greek project to define wisdom and the blessed life."

Ludwig Marcuse[84] reminds us that

"Believing is a comfort; thinking is an effort,"

---

[83] Luc Ferry is a French philosopher, politician and a proponent of secular humanism.

[84] Ludwig Marcuse was a German philosopher and writer of Jewish origin.

The philosophy moved by someone like a Spinoza, and not by simple and sterile belief, does not seem to be for every type of human being, since the comfort zone of feeling like belonging to a herd offers, is a very welcome consolation to the lazy psyche or those made incapable by the circumstances of life to seek the truth.

Homo hierarchicus cannot claim to seek the truth, as it is conditioned by the assumption that it has already found it and that it lives in its religious or ideological option.

For purposes like this, the Caste system is perfect, producing such kind of human beings. Who cares about that?

I wonder if the social contract, possible to exist in India, can only be expressed through life organized in Caste, even though today's laws prohibit them. Suppose the answer is yes; this is the only possible way to organize the collected circumstances thousands of years ago among Hindus. In that case, I think we will definitely be signing our certificate of philosophical deformity, of spiritual stupidity, which, for me, means the end of our ability to know what is decent and worthy in the life of a Human being.

ABOUT THE AUTHOR

Jan Val Ellam is the pen name of a visionary Brazilian author, Rogério de Freitas. Val Ellam wrote and published more than 40 books in his career to date, widely available in several languages on Amazon. He has also delivered hundreds of hours of lectures in Brazil and other countries. Even given his near-phenomenal output, Val Ellam feels called to write roughly 100 additional books on the phenomenal truths he's been able to uncover.

Val Ellam writes about intersecting points or convergences, especially those between Christian thought, universalist spiritualism, and planetary citizenship. In fulfillment of his mission to bring the hidden ancient history of the Human Race – whom he sees as his planetary brothers and sisters – Val Ellam has had broadcast programs on Radio Network in one of the biggest city of Brasil, Sao Paulo, and in the north of Brazil in the city of Natal, where he spoke about spirituality and planetary citizenship.

Val Ellam's work has brought to humanity information about a Cosmic Revelation, which explains how and why Earth became victim to an imposed planetary quarantine - a lock-down of cosmic proportions – and it is coming to an end - we on Earth will become reinstated into a kind of cosmic communion with our brothers and sisters across this Universe, as well as across parallel universes.

Brazil has long been a globally recognized hot spot for UFO and extraterrestrial encounters. National Enquirer reporter Bob Pratt went to Brazil on assignment and wrote a book *UFO Danger Zone*[85]. – By the time Rogério was 18 years of age, he had a positive reputation as a local UFO scholar; he was brought to Pratt's attention. Pratt asked Rogério and the warm and generous people; Brazilians opened their hearts, displayed their evidence, and gave information, as Pratt says in his book.

However, even sages and seers need day jobs, and Rogério served as an executive manager at Bank of Brazil. He had to cope with the same human judgments of all the visionaries that marked our history of all times.

One answer to this dilemma was the adoption of the pseudonym Jan Val Ellam. In this way, he kept the freedom to reveal his important truths to those in this world eager to really learn.

While the very idea of the existence of extraterrestrials and a universe-spanning civilization challenges belief, Val Ellam has made his reputation in the field as a sober yet visionary explorer into realms beyond

---

[85] *UFO Danger Zone* find these book in Amazon.

those most of us seem confined to. He became a seer, able to communicate with entities from several realms, from the dead of this world to extraphysical beings from parallel worlds – even beings from antimaterial worlds. This is where the Trimurti and other races of extraterrestrials come from.

In his explorations, Val Ellam has become an expert in our origins, starting with the god-like beings who created the master Matrix, the range of reality we all live in.

The forthcoming end of this planetary isolation is one of the highlights of his works. He is also known for his *Terra Atlantis trilogy*, an unearthing of Atlantis and its glorious heritage, only in Portuguese for now. However, perhaps his most important revelations center around *Lucifer's Rebellion*, an act of cosmic defiance that came about before our blue planet even existed.

Because he is Brazilian, most of Val Ellam's works have been published in Portuguese. However, translations, studies, and summaries of his works are becoming available at www.Pandoraunlock.com.

In this book, *The Dharma and The Hindu Castes*, Val Ellam takes a completely revealing approach with aspects never before analyzed, only because humanity is unaware of what really happened.

Val Ellam will lead us to information starting with the simple vocabulary, identifications of characters not well known by the Christian-Jewish traditions. He brought forth previously hidden revelations that make us deeply reflect how much we need to grow to face with maturity the transformations that we need to bring to the planet earth.

www.Pandoraunlock.com

Lamp Publisher

Manifesto

Val Ellam's Manifesto
A Declaration of Planetary Citizenship

We are all planetary citizens. This does not interfere with our nationality, nor with our loyalty to our individual countries. However, our planetary citizenship should never be forgotten.

We are seen as childlike because to these Cosmic races; we are a child-race, newly arrived on the Cosmic stage. We are judged harshly by the lack of indignation we display in the face of all the misery we humans are heirs to – both material and spiritual misery. To advance to the next level of individual and cultural evolution, we need to improve conditions for all of us living on the Earth.

The inner, peaceful strength we are required to embrace is an active force for positive change. This strength is soft in tolerance, never violent. Our deep inner strength is eternally demanding peace, harmony, and an urgent awareness that all of us are destined – and Cosmically-required.

Spread throughout the planet, this information – especially to new generations – will open the path that will allow us to reunite our work for a better planet Earth, here in our universe.

This manifesto is a message of hope in our ability to improve each of our Cosmic lives. Hope and faith will live in each of our abilities to continue to dignify humanity, at all levels, for all people, at all times.

Jan Val Ellam
Translation and adaptation by Helena Ribeiro

www.ingramcontent.com/pod-product-compliance
Lightning Source LLC
Chambersburg PA
CBHW071459070426
42452CB00041B/1937
* 9 7 8 1 7 3 6 5 8 3 4 0 1 *